THE HAIRY BIKERS'

MEDITERRANEAN ADVENTURE

THE HAIRY BIKERS'
MEDITERRANEAN ADVENTURE

SI KING & DAVE MYERS

SEVEN DIALS

We'd like to dedicate this book to Catherine Phipps, a remarkable writer, friend and colleague. It's a constant delight to be able to share our love of the adventure of food and our passion for discovery with her.

First published in Great Britain in 2017 by
Seven Dials, an imprint of the Orion Publishing Group Ltd
Carmelite House
50 Victoria Embankment
London EC4Y 0DZ
An Hachette UK Company

10 9 8 7 6 5 4

A CIP catalogue record for this book is available from the British Library.

ISBN: 978 1 409 17191 1

Recipe and food consultant: Catherine Phipps
Photographer: Andrew Hayes-Watkins
Food stylists: Lisa Harrison, Anna Burges-Lumsden
Design and art direction: Hart Studio
Project editor: Jinny Johnson
Prop stylist: Sarah Birks
Food stylists' assistants: Lou Kenny, Sophie Mackinnon
Proofreader: Elise See Tai
Indexer: Vicki Robinson

BBC and the BBC logo are trademarks of the British Broadcasting Corporation and are used under licence. BBC logo © BBC 1996

Printed and bound in Germany

The Orion Publishing Group's policy is to use papers that are natural, renewable and recyclable and made from wood grown in sustainable forests. The logging and manufacturing processes are expected to conform to the environmental regulations of the country of origin.

www.orionbooks.co.uk

OUR MEDITERRANEAN ADVENTURE

• •

We've spent the last few months travelling through the Mediterranean area, eating the most amazing food, seeing incredible places and meeting lovely people. Call this work? What lucky lads we are.

We've dreamed of doing a trip like this for years and finally we got the chance, but we didn't realise just how great it was all going to be. When you think of the Med you conjure up visions of blue seas, beautiful beaches and little islands, but there is so much more to it than that. The Mediterranean Sea is surrounded by 21 countries and there are more than 180 islands. We couldn't do everything on just one journey so we decided to stick to the Western Mediterranean that we know and love and concentrate on Italy, France and Spain and a few of their islands. It turned out to be the most exciting and rewarding adventure we've ever had.

And the great thing is that not only is Mediterranean food so tasty, the Mediterranean diet is also reckoned to be a really healthy one to follow – lots of fresh vegetables and fruit, herbs, pulses, fish and meat; and lots and lots of olive oil. This is not a diet book, but we agree that the Mediterraneans have a great way of eating. And to prove the point, in Sardinia we found one of the world's famous Blue Zones – places where a much higher than average number of people live to over a hundred. There's a cluster of villages in Sardinia that are full of centenarians. We went to visit and cook with them and what do you think we found? They eat a diet that's rich in lard because it's a good cheap way of getting in lots of calories, which they need for their hard-working life on the land. Of course, they have loads of fresh veg, pulses and other good stuff as well.

We thought we knew these countries well but there was so much to discover. We wanted to find the real Mediterranean and experience it in a way we hadn't ever before. The area has an incredibly rich and varied history, with Greek, Roman, Moorish and other invaders and conquerors criss-crossing the waters of the Med over the last few thousand years and all have left their mark. The Med is a superhighway for history, culture and food and we found that when you scratch beneath the surface, Mediterranean cuisine isn't all one and the same – it is a distillation of many cultures and traditions and still as varied as the countries themselves. And it is amazing that these influences haven't been lost. They are alive and well – you can still taste them in the food. We have never sampled any other cuisine that is so born out of its environment.

We started our journey in southern Italy, in Puglia and Calabria, where we ate some of the best – and simplest – food we came across during the whole trip. We moved on to the wild and rugged islands of Sardinia and Corsica and then to the South of France. From there we travelled to the Balearic Islands of Menorca and Mallorca and on to southern Spain, where our journey ended – for now.

What we found is that despite their different histories, these lands are united by their attitude to food and the theme that ran right through our journey was seasonal, fresh, natural and simple. We always felt like we were getting the freshest and best of ingredients everywhere we went. It was like eating sunshine all day long and it made us smile.

We felt that the countries we visited must be the best places on Earth to live and we were touched by the genuine friendliness and generosity of everyone we met, from the people running the farms, restaurants and cafés where we filmed, to the fishermen on the beaches and the stallholders in the markets. Everyone was welcoming and so eager to talk to us about what they liked to cook and eat.

We learned so much about food. We found that much of Mediterranean cooking is instinctive and handed down from generation to generation and that's what keeps the traditions alive. There's a way of doing things because that's how they've always been done, and people stick to that rather than always striving for something new. It's also about eating what's available at any given time of year and showing the utmost respect for the ingredients. Mediterranean people have a deep interest in food. They don't eat to live, they live to eat. We watched shoppers in the market carefully inspecting every tomato, every piece of fish, before buying. They look forward to cooking and eating. Mealtimes are all about family and celebration, not just fuel.

The Mediterranean climate, the sun and the soil provide people with the most incredible environment to produce the food they eat. If you have just a scrap of land you can grow some of the best food in the world and talking to people we felt that if they could grow and pick everything they ate, they would. The produce is so good you don't always need to do much to it. In one bar in Italy we sat and ate broad beans straight from the pod with our drinks and we'd never appreciated their flavour more.

All the way from Puglia to Torremolinos we found food to enjoy and celebrate – food to rejoice in and that made us feel good. We were intoxicated by the experiences we had and we can't wait to go back. At one point in a beautiful spot in Andalucia, near the end of our journey, Dick our director turned to us and said: 'This must be heaven, mustn't it?' We think he's right.

Love Si and Dave

SOUTHERN ITALY

Puglia and Calabria, in the 'heel' and 'toe' of Italy, are some of the poorest parts of the country and this is where we started our journey. Way back in the 8th century BC, these lands were occupied by the Greeks and the local dialect in some parts is still basically Ancient Greek. Even now, road signs in parts of Calabria are in Greek as well as Italian.

The food there was some of the best we had on our whole trip and it was simplicity itself. The culinary tradition there is known as 'cucina povera' – rustic food for the poor – and was born of the need to make the best of cheap, simple, everyday ingredients and waste nothing. We met a chef called Giuseppe and he cooked us a dish of chickpeas and pasta – we just couldn't get enough of it. Then we found ourselves waxing lyrical about turnip tops and chilli served with orecchiette, an ear-shaped pasta that's traditional in Puglia. It was truly great food but there was nothing fancy, nothing expensive. When we told Giuseppe how much we enjoyed his dishes he just shrugged – it was normal food to him, just what he ate every day. Lucky man.

In Calabria we sampled some of the local sweet-tasting onions, known as tropea onions, which were brought there by the Greeks. We used them to make an excellent frittata. And we learned how to make the spicy pork paste known as n'duja from an 85-year-old Calabrian lady and added some to an amazing Italian-American stromboli pizza. Wow!

CAPRESE SALAD

SERVES 4 AS A STARTER OR SIDE

This salad is simplicity itself but it is a stunning dish. It does depend on good tomatoes though so is best made in summer when they have lots of flavour. Always use tomatoes that are at room temperature or warmed by the sun – never fridge cold. If possible, use a mix of different colours and varieties, including some cherry tomatoes. Don't be tempted to mess it about with pesto or other bits and bobs, though. Keep this classic . . . well, classic!

500g tomatoes (mix of colours and types), at room temperature

2 balls of fresh mozzarella, drained

3–4 tbsp extra virgin olive oil

handful of basil leaves

salt and black pepper

Slice the larger tomatoes and halve or quarter the smaller ones. Arrange them all on a large serving platter or on 4 individual plates. Slice or tear the mozzarella into bite-sized pieces and tuck them in and around the tomato slices.

Drizzle over the olive oil, then add the basil leaves, tearing any large ones. Season well with salt and black pepper and serve.

ARANCINI

RISOTTO BALLS

MAKES 12

These little beauties are Dave's favourite – balls of risotto, stuffed with mozzarella and basil, then coated with breadcrumbs and deep-fried. Yum, is what we say. You can make the rice from scratch as we've done here, or use leftover risotto – you'll need about 600g.

1 tbsp olive oil

15g butter

1 medium onion, finely chopped

1 garlic clove, finely chopped

zest of ½ lemon

150g risotto rice

pinch of saffron, soaked in a little warm water

50ml vermouth or white wine

600ml chicken stock

25g Parmesan, grated

salt and black pepper

Filling

1 large ball of mozzarella, cut into 12 cubes (about 150g)

12 basil leaves

Coating and cooking

2 eggs

50g flour

100g fine breadcrumbs

vegetable oil, for deep-frying

Heat the oil and butter in a large, shallow pan. When the butter has melted and is foaming, add the onion and cook it over a low heat until it has softened. Add the garlic, zest and rice and cook for a further minute until the rice is glossy and translucent. Pour in the saffron with its soaking water and the vermouth or wine. Bring to the boil and let the liquid bubble away until it's almost completely absorbed. Turn the heat down to medium and start adding the stock, a ladleful at a time. Stir continuously, allowing all the liquid to be absorbed before adding more. It should take about 20 minutes to add all the liquid. At this stage the rice should be cooked but still have a little bite. Season and beat in the Parmesan.

Allow the risotto to cool to room temperature, then chill – this will make the rice firmer and easier to work with. Wrap each mozzarella cube in a basil leaf and set it aside. Wet your hands, take a heaped tablespoon of rice (about 50g) and make a dip in the centre. Press a mozzarella cube into the dip, then smooth the rice back over it. Repeat until you have used up all the rice and filling.

Beat one of the eggs in a bowl. Spread half the flour over a plate and half the breadcrumbs over another plate. Start rolling the arancini in the flour, then dust off the excess. Dip them in the egg, then roll in the breadcrumbs and set them aside. When you have coated about half of them, add the rest of the egg, flour and breadcrumbs to the plates and continue.

Half fill a large saucepan or deep-fat fryer with oil. Heat the oil to 170°C or test the temperature by frying a cube of bread – it should turn light brown in about 30 seconds. Fry the arancini, about 4 at a time, for 4–5 minutes until deep golden brown. Serve at once. You can bake the arancini if you prefer. Preheat the oven to 180°C/Fan 160°C/Gas 4. Put the coated arancini on a baking tray, drizzle them with oil and bake for about 20 minutes. Great with a tomato and basil salad.

BRUSCHETTA

BOTH FILLINGS MAKE ENOUGH FOR 4

This is basically tasty things on toast – Italian style! It probably originated in Rome but is popular all over the Mediterranean area and is the perfect starter or snack to serve with drinks. Try our ideas, then let your imagination run riot and come up with some of your own. Ricotta is a soft Italian cheese and is available in supermarkets. For the tomato version, make sure you get great tomatoes and serve them at room temperature.

4 slices of rustic
sourdough bread
(about 1.5cm thick)
1 garlic clove, cut in half
salt and black pepper

Tomato bruschetta

4–6 very ripe tomatoes,
at room temperature
a few basil leaves,
shredded
2 tbsp olive oil

**Ricotta and broad
bean bruschetta**

200g broad beans
(podded weight)
250g ricotta
juice and zest of 1 lemon
2 tbsp olive oil
a few small mint leaves
a few basil leaves,
shredded

Toast the bread to a light golden brown. Take the garlic halves and rub the cut side over the toast.

For the tomato bruschetta, roughly chop the tomatoes and put them in a bowl. Add most of the basil leaves, reserving a few for a garnish, and the olive oil. Season with a generous amount of salt and some black pepper. Stir and leave the tomatoes to stand for a few minutes.

Divide the tomato mixture between the slices of toast and garnish with a few more torn basil leaves. Serve at room temperature.

For the ricotta and broad bean bruschetta, bring a saucepan of water to the boil and cook the broad beans for about 2 minutes. Drain, run them under cold water, then remove their skins.

Break up the ricotta with a fork and add the lemon juice. Stir to combine, then spread this mixture over the toasted bread. Drizzle with a tablespoon of the olive oil. Toss the broad beans with the mint and basil leaves reserving a few for a garnish, then add the lemon zest and the remaining olive oil. Mix thoroughly and pile this on top of the ricotta. Season with salt and pepper and serve immediately.

CIALLEDDA SALAD

TOMATO AND BREAD SALAD

SERVES 4

This is a traditional salad in Puglia, southern Italy, and is similar to the Tuscan panzanella. Both are a great way of using up stale bread, which soaks up the delicious juices of the tomatoes and dressing, but this one is even more frugal and we reckon better. Use the best oil you can afford, as you really notice the difference in this salad.

about 200g stale ciabatta or good sourdough-type bread

1 small red onion, very finely sliced

500g very ripe tomatoes

1 garlic clove, crushed

½ tsp dried oregano

2 tbsp extra virgin olive oil

handful of black olives

small bunch of basil

salt and black pepper

Tear or cut the bread into chunks of about 3–4cm. Sprinkle them with a little water – just enough to moisten the surface. You don't want the bread to get too sodden as it will also soak up some of the tomato juices.

Sprinkle the red onion slices with salt and put them in a bowl of cold water for half an hour – this reduces the bitterness. Drain the slices and set them aside.

Roughly chop the tomatoes and put them in a serving bowl, together with any juices released when you're chopping. Add the garlic and oregano and season well with salt and pepper.

Drizzle over the olive oil, then add the bread, drained onion, olives and basil. Leave the salad to stand for half an hour at room temperature before serving.

BURRATA, PARMA HAM

AND GRILLED PEACH SALAD

SERVES 4 AS A STARTER, 2 FOR A MAIN MEAL

Burrata is a very special cheese that comes from Puglia. It's like mozzarella that's been to finishing school and it's rich and luxurious. If you can't find any, use mozzarella instead, but with burrata this has to be one of the best salads ever. It was worth the trip to the Med for this dish alone.

½ red onion, sliced into crescents

3 peaches, cut into wedges

1 tsp olive oil, plus 2 tbsp

100g rocket or other salad leaves

100g Parma ham, sliced

1 large burrata (or 2 mozzarella)

2 tsp balsamic vinegar

handful of basil leaves

salt and black pepper

Add salt to a bowl of cold water and then the slices of red onion. Leave them to soak for half an hour, then drain thoroughly.

Next grill the peaches. Heat a griddle pan until it's too hot to hold your hand over comfortably. Toss the peach wedges in a teaspoon of olive oil, then griddle them on each cut side until charred with black grill marks – this should take about 2–3 minutes on each side. Set them aside to cool slightly.

Arrange the leaves on a serving plate or in individual salad bowls. Add the Parma ham, peach wedges and red onions, then break the burrata into pieces and add them too. Drizzle over 2 tablespoons of olive oil, followed by the balsamic vinegar and season lightly with salt and pepper. Garnish with the basil leaves.

STUFFED AUBERGINES

SERVES 4

This is a classic example of the 'cucina povera' tradition in this part of the world – the rustic food of the poor. Such dishes use simple ingredients to cook meals that are cheap to make but full of flavour. The more expensive ingredients, such as cheese, are bulked out with breadcrumbs and herbs.

4 large aubergines

6 tbsp olive oil

1 large onion, finely chopped

3 garlic cloves, finely chopped

1 tsp dried thyme

1 tsp dried oregano

pinch of chilli flakes (optional)

4 medium tomatoes, skinned and chopped

50g white breadcrumbs (ciabatta is good)

25g Parmesan or Pecorino cheese, grated

zest of ½ lemon

handful of basil leaves, shredded

salt and black pepper

Preheat the oven to 200°C/Fan 180°C/Gas 6. Cut the aubergines in half lengthways. Leaving a border of about ½cm, cut out the flesh from each half, dice it and set it aside. Brush the inside of the aubergines with olive oil and season them with salt. Place them in a baking tin and cover with foil, then bake for 20 minutes.

Meanwhile, heat 2 tablespoons of the olive oil in a saucepan. Add the onion and sauté it gently over a medium heat for 10 minutes until well softened. Turn up the heat, then add the garlic and aubergine flesh and stir until the aubergine has lightly browned. Add the herbs and chilli flakes, if using, then the tomatoes and season with salt and pepper. Stir to combine, then reduce the heat and cover the pan. Simmer for 10 minutes, then remove the lid and continue to cook until any liquid has evaporated.

Remove the aubergines from the oven – leave the oven on – and fill them with the stuffing. Mix the breadcrumbs with the cheese, lemon zest and basil, then season with a little salt and pepper. Sprinkle this mixture over the stuffed aubergines, then drizzle with more olive oil.

Bake the aubergines, uncovered, for 25–30 minutes until the filling is hot and the top has lightly browned.

ONION FRITTATA

SERVES 2-4

We cooked this in Calabria when we were filming there and we used the wonderful local tropea onions, which were actually brought to Italy by the Greeks. They're sweet, crunchy and said to be an aphrodisiac! We were told the best way to eat them was in an omelette so that's what we did, but we added loads of fresh herbs too. Awesome. In the UK, use any nice sweet red onions.

2 tbsp olive oil

600g red onions, thinly sliced (about 5 medium)

6 eggs

50g Parmesan, finely grated

3–4 tbsp finely chopped fresh herbs, such as marjoram, oregano, mint and basil

15g butter

salt and black pepper

Heat the oil in a large frying pan and add the onions. Cover the pan and cook the onions over a very low heat for 25–30 minutes, stirring every so often, until they have collapsed down. Turn up the heat to medium and continue to cook the onions for another 10 minutes until they're lightly caramelised and a rich golden brown – keep stirring regularly. Remove the pan from the heat.

Crack the eggs into a bowl and beat them well. Stir in the cooked onions, cheese and herbs and season with salt and pepper.

Preheat your grill to a low setting. Melt the butter in a non-stick frying pan over a medium heat. When it is foaming, turn down the heat and pour in the egg and onion mixture, making sure the onion is evenly spread. Cook the frittata for several minutes – up to 10 – until the eggs are almost set. Put the pan under the preheated grill until the eggs are set but don't let the frittata take on too much colour – watch it very carefully.

Leave the frittata to cool for a few minutes, then run a spatula around the edge and turn it out on to a plate. Cut it into wedges and serve at room temperature.

ROAST CAULIFLOWER
WITH SPICED ANCHOVY SAUCE
SERVES 4 AS A SIDE DISH OR STARTER

This spicy sauce makes a great dip for serving with sticks of raw veg and would also be nice with raw or griddled wedges of endive. It's very similar to a dish called anchoiade, popular in the South of France. Good to see the humble cauli take centre stage.

1 large cauliflower, broken into small florets
2 tbsp olive oil
25g pine nuts
2 tbsp roughly chopped flatleaf parsley
1 tbsp basil leaves, finely shredded

Anchovy sauce
1 x 50g can of anchovy fillets, drained and the oil reserved
zest and juice of 1 lemon
2 garlic cloves, crushed
½–1 tsp chilli flakes
50ml olive oil
salt and black pepper

Preheat the oven to 200°C/Fan 180°C/Gas 6. Put the cauliflower in a bowl and drizzle over the olive oil. Toss the cauliflower until it is well coated with the oil, then spread it over a baking tray or roasting tin. Roast it in the oven for 25–30 minutes, until cooked but still with a bit of bite to it. It should be lightly browned with the occasional charred patch.

Meanwhile, make the sauce. Put the anchovies in a small food processor with the lemon zest and juice, the garlic and chilli flakes. Season with pepper only at this stage – the anchovies are very salty. Whizz everything together. Add olive oil to the oil reserved from the anchovy fillets, making the quantity up to 75ml. While the motor is running, drizzle in the oil until you have a thick, emulsified sauce. Taste for seasoning and add a little salt if you think it needs it.

Arrange the cauliflower in a serving dish or platter. Toast the pine nuts lightly in a dry frying pan and sprinkle these among the cauliflower along with the parsley and basil. Serve with the sauce on the side.

FRIGGITELLI EGGS

EGGS WITH PEPPERS

SERVES 4

Friggitelli peppers are the small, light green to red ones, which are thinner-fleshed than the regular bell peppers. They're pretty easy to get hold of now but you can use bell peppers instead if you like. This makes a great breakfast and reminds us of the trendy Israeli dish, shakshuka.

500g friggitelli peppers or similar

3 tbsp olive oil

2 garlic cloves, finely chopped

2 medium tomatoes, peeled and finely chopped

pinch of cayenne

4–8 eggs (1 or 2 per person)

squeeze of lemon juice

salt and black pepper

To serve

basil leaves

slices of crusty country bread, toasted

Cut the peppers in half and cut out the cores and membranes. Slice them into 1 cm strips, lengthways. Heat 2 tablespoons of the oil in a large frying pan and sauté the pepper strips over a medium heat until they are tender, but haven't lost their shape. Add the garlic and cook for another couple of minutes. Add the tomatoes with a splash of water and the cayenne, then season with salt and pepper. Simmer, uncovered, for 10 minutes, until the tomatoes have broken down and reduced, then remove the pan from the heat and let everything cool slightly.

Heat the remaining oil in a large frying pan. Add the eggs and fry until the whites are completely cooked but the yolks are nice and soft. Season them with a little salt and squeeze over some lemon juice.

Serve the peppers in the centre of each plate with the eggs placed on top. The yolk will break through and coat the peppers when you cut into it. Sprinkle over a few small basil leaves and serve with toasted bread.

PETTOLE

STUFFED DOUGH BALLS

MAKES ABOUT 24

We made these little goodies with Chef Giuseppe in Puglia. They're stuffed with veg and can be fried or baked. The baked pettole are easier, as you just have to shove them in the oven, but we recommend adding the topping to make them really yummy. The fried version doesn't need it.

Filling
1 tbsp olive oil

½ small courgette (about 50g), finely diced

1 garlic clove, finely chopped

½ roasted red pepper (see p.320), finely diced

4 sun-blushed tomatoes, finely chopped

a few basil leaves, shredded

salt and black pepper

Dough
250g strong white flour, plus extra for dusting

1 tsp instant yeast

1 tsp salt

1 tbsp olive oil

150ml tepid water

To cook
vegetable oil, for deep-frying (optional)

Topping (optional)
2 tbsp olive oil

2 garlic cloves, sliced

First prepare the filling. Heat the olive oil in a frying pan. Add the courgette and fry it over a fairly high heat, stirring regularly, until lightly browned on all sides. Add the garlic and cook for a couple more minutes. Remove the pan from the heat and stir in the pepper, tomatoes and basil. Season to taste and leave to cool.

To make the dough, mix the flour, yeast and salt in a large bowl. Drizzle in the olive oil and stir in the vegetables. Pour in the water and mix to form a rather sticky dough. Turn the dough out on to a floured work surface and knead until smooth – the dough will turn a rich shade of orange. Shape it into a large ball, then place it in a lightly oiled bowl and cover with cling film or a damp tea towel. Leave the dough to prove for an hour until doubled in size.

Turn the dough out on to a floured work surface and cut it into 24 pieces (about 20g each). Shape each piece into a ball by pulling the sides into the centre repeatedly until it tightens into a round. Place the pieces on a baking tray to prove for another 20 minutes until they have puffed up slightly and are springy to touch.

To bake the pettole, preheat the oven to 220°C/Fan 200°C/Gas 7 and cook them for 15–20 minutes until they are golden brown and sound hollow when tapped. Alternatively, to deep-fry, half fill a saucepan or deep-fat fryer with oil. Heat the oil to 170°C. Add the balls a few at a time and fry them for 5–7 minutes until they are a rich golden brown, flipping them over half way through.

For the topping, if using, heat the oil in a frying pan and add the garlic. Cook it very gently for 2–3 minutes – don't let it colour – then remove with a slotted spoon. Brush the garlicky oil over the dough balls and sprinkle with salt.

CAPONATA

SERVES 4

No, we haven't gone mad – the chocolate in this recipe is traditional and adds a lovely richness. For us, caponata is a must on any Mediterranean table. We like to use fresh tomatoes as they cook down in a creamier way than the canned and the dish is better for that. The other thing we like about this version is that the aubergines aren't cooked for too long so they aren't sludgy. See what you think, but we reckon this is good.

3 large aubergines, diced into 2cm cubes

1 tbsp salt

100ml olive oil, plus extra if needed

1 large red onion, sliced into wedges

3 celery sticks, thinly sliced

400g fresh plum tomatoes, peeled and finely diced

½ tsp chilli flakes (optional)

50g green olives (unpitted weight), pitted and sliced

25g capers, rinsed

2–3 tbsp red wine vinegar

1 tsp caster sugar

10g dark chocolate (optional)

salt and black pepper

To serve

small bunch of basil leaves, roughly torn

Put the aubergine cubes in a colander and sprinkle them with a tablespoon of salt. Leave them to stand for half an hour in the sink or over a bowl, then pat them dry. Heat the olive oil in a large frying pan and fry the aubergine cubes in batches until they are a rich brown all over. Make sure they are completely cooked as they will not get much cooking time at the later stage.

When you have fried all the aubergine, there should be some oil left in the pan, but if there isn't, add a couple more tablespoons. Add the red onion and celery and cook them quite briskly for several minutes, until they are softened but still al dente. Add the tomatoes and chilli flakes, if using, and season with salt and pepper. Simmer for 5 minutes, then add the olives, capers, 2 tablespoons of the red wine vinegar, the sugar and the chocolate, if using. Simmer very gently for another 10 minutes. Taste and add more red wine vinegar if you like.

Add the aubergines to the pan and stir until they are fully coated with the sauce. Let everything simmer for just 2 minutes, then remove the pan from the heat. Check for seasoning and add salt and pepper if necessary. Leave to cool to room temperature and serve, sprinkled with fresh basil.

ORECCHIETTE

WITH GREENS

SERVES 4

A traditional dish in Puglia, this is usually made with greens called cime di rapa, also called turnip tops, or with wild broccoli, which has a nice, slightly bitter flavour. In the UK we can use sprouting broccoli, kale or cavolo nero. Orecchiette are a popular pasta in the region and their shape resembles little ears, hence the name which comes from the Italian word for ear – orecchio. You can find the dried version in supermarkets but if you can't find any, use any short pasta such as small shells or penne. This dish really summed up 'cucina povera' for us and was one of the simplest, nicest things we have ever tasted – honest! Traditionally it's not served with cheese but we like a bit of Parmesan or Pecorino on top – we'll leave it to you to decide.

400g orecchiette or other short pasta

500g cime di rapa, sprouting broccoli, kale or cavolo nero

3 tbsp olive oil

4 garlic cloves, finely chopped

1 tsp chilli flakes

zest of ½ lemon

Parmesan or Pecorino cheese, grated, to serve (optional)

salt and black pepper

Bring a large saucepan of salted water to the boil. Add the pasta and cook until just al dente.

While the pasta is cooking, prepare the sauce. Chop up the greens into 4–5cm lengths, discarding any really tough stems. Put them in a saucepan and add water to a depth of about 3cm. Season with salt, then bring to the boil and cover. Simmer for 4–5 minutes until the greens are tender and the leaves have wilted down. The colour should still be very fresh and green.

Drain the greens. Heat the olive oil in a large frying pan and sauté the garlic for a minute or so – you don't want it to take on any colour. Add the greens along with the chilli flakes and lemon zest. Check for seasoning and add a little more salt and some pepper if necessary.

When the pasta is cooked, reserve a couple of ladlefuls of the cooking liquid and drain the pasta. Add 3–4 tablespoons of the reserved liquid to the greens, just to moisten, then add the pasta. Swirl everything around the pan for a minute or so, then serve immediately with grated cheese, if using.

BUCATINI CON LE SARDE

PASTA WITH SARDINES

SERVES 4

Bucatini is one of our favourite pastas. It's quite thick but with a hollow centre and works brilliantly with this sauce, but you can use ordinary spaghetti if you like. The sardine sauce is a southern Italian classic and is super tasty. It's great with fresh or canned fish.

4 tbsp olive oil
1 large fennel bulb, with feathery fronds
50g raisins
1 tbsp red wine vinegar
50g pine nuts or flaked almonds
300g sardine fillets, cut into bite-sized pieces
4 anchovy fillets, finely chopped
a pinch of saffron, soaked in 2 tbsp warm water
400g bucatini
salt and black pepper

To serve
2 tbsp olive oil
25g fresh breadcrumbs
pinch of chilli flakes (optional)

Heat the olive oil in a large, lidded frying pan. Trim the fennel, then dice it finely, reserving any fronds, and add it to the olive oil with a generous pinch of salt. Fry it over a medium to high heat for 10 minutes to soften and start the caramelising process, then add a splash of water and cover the pan. Turn down the heat and leave the fennel to soften for a further 5 minutes.

Put the raisins in a small saucepan and add the vinegar and 2 tablespoons of water. Bring it to the boil, then remove the pan from the heat and leave the raisins to soften. Lightly toast the nuts in a dry frying pan.

Add the pine nuts or almonds, the raisins, sardines and anchovies to the fennel. Cook over a low heat, stirring regularly, for 5 minutes. Add the saffron and its water and stir to combine.

Make the garnish. Heat the olive oil in a small saucepan. Add the breadcrumbs and the chilli flakes, if using, and plenty of salt and pepper. Fry briskly until the breadcrumbs are crisp and golden.

Meanwhile, bring a large pot of salted water to the boil and cook the bucatini. Add a ladleful of the cooking water to the fennel and sardine sauce, then drain the pasta. Add the pasta to the sauce in the pan and cook for a couple more minutes. Serve with the fried breadcrumbs and reserved fennel fronds sprinkled on top.

PESTOS

EACH SERVES 4 WITH PASTA

Over the years, jars of pesto have found their way into all our store cupboards and fridges, but there's nothing as good as home-made. Pesto is so easy to make and just bursts with life and flavour. It's one of those culinary marvels that never lets you down. Here are a couple of different versions to try – the classic and another made with pistachios.

Classic pesto

50g pine nuts
50g basil leaves (from one large bunch)
1 garlic clove, crushed
100ml olive oil
25g Parmesan, grated
salt and black pepper

Pistachio pesto

50g pistachios
25g flatleaf parsley leaves
25g basil leaves
1 garlic clove, crushed
zest and juice of 1 lemon
100ml olive oil
salt and black pepper

To store

extra olive oil

For the classic basil pesto, put the pine nuts in a frying pan and toast them over a medium heat. Shake the pan regularly and watch the pine nuts carefully. When they are lightly coloured and you can smell their aroma, remove the pan from the heat and tip the nuts on to a plate to cool.

Pound the basil in a pestle and mortar with a pinch of salt, a coarse grinding of black pepper and the garlic. When the basil has completely broken down, add the nuts and continue to pound until they are finely crushed. Stir in the oil and Parmesan, then taste and add more seasoning if needed.

Alternatively, put the nuts and herbs in a food processor until very finely chopped, then add the rest of the ingredients. Pulse briefly but do not overwork, as this shouldn't be a smooth sauce. It needs texture. This pesto, and the pistachio version below, can be used immediately or put in a jar, covered with a layer of olive oil and stored in the fridge.

For the pistachio pesto, put the nuts in a bowl and cover them with just-boiled water. Leave them to stand for 3–4 minutes. Drain them thoroughly, tip them on to a tea towel and rub them vigorously. The skins should slip off easily. Discard the skins. Put the nuts in a dry frying pan and toast them over a medium heat, shaking the pan regularly, until they're very lightly coloured and smelling wonderful. Remove the pan from the heat and put the nuts on a plate to cool.

It's best to make this pesto with a food processor, as parsley tends to be coarser than basil and harder to pound to a paste. Put the herbs and pistachios in the food processor until very finely chopped, then add the rest of the ingredients. Pulse briefly – do not overwork – leave some texture. Taste and add salt and black pepper if necessary.

SPAGHETTI
WITH ANCHOVIES,
BREADCRUMBS AND CHILLI
SERVES 4

This is the real deal – one of those pasta dishes that's so tasty and simple you want to go on eating forever. Sometimes we can be guilty of trying too hard with a dish and we know this one needs nothing more. Put Pavarotti on the player – we feel some Traviata coming on.

5 tbsp olive oil
1 garlic clove, crushed
50g can of anchovies, drained and finely chopped
pinch of chilli flakes
50g breadcrumbs from a country-style loaf, not too fine
2 tbsp finely chopped flatleaf parsley
2 tbsp finely shredded basil
salt and black pepper
400g spaghetti

To make the sauce, put 4 tablespoons of the oil in a large frying pan and add the garlic. Cook it very gently for 3–4 minutes, then add the anchovies. Mash the anchovies into the oil until they are puréed and completely combined with the garlic, then add the chilli flakes. Season with black pepper – do not add salt. Stir the sauce, remove the pan from the heat and set it aside.

Heat the remaining oil in a separate frying pan, then add the breadcrumbs and season them with salt and pepper. Cook the crumbs over a medium heat, stirring regularly, until they are lightly coloured, then tip them into a bowl. Stir in the herbs.

Cook the spaghetti in plenty of salted water for 10–12 minutes until al dente. Towards the end of the cooking time, when the cooking water has plenty of starch in it, add a ladleful of the water to the pan of sauce. Reheat the sauce gently.

Drain the pasta, then add it to the sauce and toss to coat the pasta. Serve with the bowl of breadcrumbs and herbs on the side so everyone can sprinkle some over their bowl of pasta.

PASTA E CECI

PASTA WITH CHICKPEAS

SERVES 4

On our first day of filming in Puglia, we went to a little trattoria run by Chef Giuseppe to try some of his 'cucina povera'. This traditional dish, made with chickpeas and fresh pasta trimmings, was sublime. It came from the need to use up leftover pasta trimmings – nothing could be wasted – and some was boiled and the rest fried, giving great texture and flavour. Giuseppe kept his version plain, but we've suggested adding anchovies and/or pancetta to the sauce. He always uses dried chickpeas and cooks them with loads of herbs – you could use canned but the dish won't be as good.

Chickpeas (or use 2 cans)

200g dried chickpeas

4 garlic cloves, cut in half

1 onion, chopped

1 carrot, chopped

2 sprigs of rosemary

2 sprigs of flatleaf parsley

1 tsp salt

1.5 litres vegetable or chicken stock

Sauce

4 tbsp olive oil

100g pancetta, finely chopped or 50g can of anchovies, drained and finely chopped (optional)

1 onion, finely chopped

1 celery stick, finely chopped

2 garlic cloves

sprig of rosemary, finely chopped

2 medium tomatoes, peeled and finely chopped

salt and black pepper

Pasta

300g fresh pasta (see p.309), cut into short 2cm strips or random small shapes

2 tbsp olive oil

Put the chickpeas in a bowl, cover them with cold water and leave to soak overnight. The next day, drain and rinse them and put them in a saucepan with the garlic, onion, carrot, herbs, salt and stock. Bring to the boil and cook fiercely for 10 minutes, then turn the heat down to medium and cook the chickpeas until they're tender – anything from 45 minutes to an hour and a half, depending on how fresh they are. Top up the stock with water if it starts to get a bit low. Once cooked, the chickpeas should keep their shape but be creamy and easy to crush.

Drain the chickpeas, reserving the liquid. Heat the oil in a frying pan. Add the pancetta or anchovies, if using, and fry for a couple of minutes. Add the onion and celery and cook until the onion is soft and translucent, then add the garlic, rosemary and tomatoes. Cook for another few minutes until any liquid from the tomatoes has evaporated, then season. Take half of the chickpeas and purée them with 600ml of the cooking liquid (or water if using canned). The consistency should be quite rough – don't make it completely smooth. Mix this with the whole chickpeas and add them to the frying pan with the sauce. Simmer for about 10 minutes until the liquid has reduced and the texture is creamy.

Cook two-thirds of the pasta in plenty of salted water until al dente. Drain it thoroughly, then mix it in with the chickpeas. Heat the olive oil in a separate frying pan, add the rest of the pasta and fry it for 3–4 minutes on each side until golden and puffed up. Drain it on kitchen paper. Serve the chickpeas and cooked pasta in bowls and garnish with the fried pasta.

PIZZETTE

MAKES 4 MEDIUM OR 6 SMALL

These little pizzas are much easier to handle than big ones and are a good starting point if you've never made pizzas before. The white version is nice made with blue cheese such as Gorgonzola if you fancy a change. Next step is that wood-fired oven that you've been dreaming about.

Pizza dough

250g strong white bread flour, plus extra for dusting

1 tsp instant yeast

1 tsp salt

150ml tepid water

1 tbsp olive oil

Puttanesca sauce

2 tbsp tomato paste

1 garlic clove, crushed

2 tbsp olive oil

large pinch of chilli flakes

large pinch of sugar

½ tsp dried oregano

a few basil leaves, finely shredded

salt and black pepper

Puttanesca topping

2 tomatoes, finely chopped and drained

1 can of anchovies, drained and split lengthways

25g capers, drained and rinsed

50g pitted olives, sliced

a few basil leaves

First make the dough. Mix the flour and yeast together in a large bowl and add the teaspoon of salt. Make a well in the centre and gradually work in the water and the olive oil, until the mixture comes together as a dough. Turn the dough out on to a floured work surface and knead until it is smooth and springy – this will take about 10 minutes. If you prefer, you can knead the dough in a stand mixer with the dough hook for 5 minutes. Put the dough in a clean, lightly oiled bowl and cover it with cling film or a damp tea towel. Leave somewhere warm until it has doubled in size.

Preheat the oven to its highest temperature. Place a couple of upturned baking trays in the oven to heat.

Turn the dough out and knock it back. For the small pizzette, divide the dough into 6 pieces, or for slightly larger ones, divide it into 4. Shape the pieces into balls, then roll out each piece thinly, stretching it out until it stops springing back.

For the puttanesca pizzette, mix all the sauce ingredients together and season with salt and pepper. Divide the sauce between the pizzette, leaving a narrow 1cm border around the edges. Then add the topping – sprinkle with the chopped tomatoes, drape over the anchovy fillets, then top with the capers, olives and basil leaves. Finish with another drizzle of olive oil if you like.

For the white pizzette, bring a saucepan of water to the boil and add salt. Add the potato slices and blanch them for 1 minute, then drain them thoroughly and pat them dry. Thinly slice the mozzarella and arrange it over the pizzette, then top with the potato slices, herbs and Parmesan shavings. Season with a little salt and pepper and drizzle with olive oil.

White topping

4 small new or waxy
potatoes (Charlotte or
Pink Fir), very thinly sliced

1 ball of mozzarella

a few sprigs of thyme OR
a few small sage leaves

a few thin shavings
of Parmesan

up to 1 tbsp olive oil

Garnish for white pizzette (optional)

50g rocket

1 tbsp olive oil

squeeze of lemon juice

Dust the baking trays with a little flour and carefully place the pizzette on the trays. Cook them for 6–7 minutes until they are lightly crisped around the edges and dappled brown.

If you are using the rocket garnish for the white pizzette, toss the rocket in the olive oil and lemon juice and season with salt and pepper. Put a small amount on top of the pizzette just before serving.

N'DUJA STROMBOLI

SERVES 4

Think pizza roly poly – this is a Hairy Bikers' finger-licking keeper. Stromboli is an American invention but the spicy pork paste known as n'duja is pure southern Italy and quite ridiculously good. We made our own n'duja in Calabria and discovered that it consists of chillies, pork fat and salt, which is then smoked. Some versions are spicier than others, so be sure to taste before you add the whole 200g.

Dough

450g strong white flour, plus extra for dusting

50g fine semolina

7g instant yeast

1 tsp salt

300ml tepid water

2 tbsp olive oil

Filling

1 large or 2 small courgettes

2 tbsp olive oil

150–200g n'duja

200g mozzarella

1 tsp dried oregano (or 1 tbsp fresh oregano leaves)

small bunch of basil, leaves only

salt and black pepper

Mix the flour, semolina and yeast together in a large bowl and add the salt. Make a well in the centre and gradually work in the water and the olive oil until the mixture comes together. Turn the dough out on to a floured work surface and knead until it is smooth and springy – this will take about 10 minutes. Put the dough in a lightly oiled bowl and cover it with cling film or a damp tea towel. Leave somewhere warm until it has doubled in size.

Meanwhile, prepare the filling. Very thinly slice the courgette on the diagonal. Toss it in a tablespoon of the olive oil and season with salt and pepper. Heat a griddle pan until it is very hot – it should be too hot to hold your hand over. Turn the heat down slightly and grill the courgette for 2–4 minutes on each side until soft and marked with char lines.

Preheat the oven to 200°C/Fan 180°C/Gas 6. Turn the bread dough out on to a lightly floured surface. Roll it out, stretching it constantly as it springs back, until you have a rectangle measuring about 45 x 30cm. Arrange the slices of courgette over the dough, leaving a 2cm border along the short and one of the long sides. Top with spoonfuls of n'duja and roughly torn mozzarella. Sprinkle over the herbs and season with salt and pepper.

Roll up the dough, starting with the borderless edge, which will be the centre of the stromboli, and pressing the short edges together as you go. Place it on a baking tray and brush it with the remaining oil. Leave it to stand for 30 minutes, covered with a damp tea towel. When the dough has risen again, put the stromboli in the oven and bake it for 25–30 minutes until golden brown. Leave it to cool for a few minutes, then cut into thick slices.

SEAFOOD
WITH COUSCOUS
SERVES 4

This is a southern Italian recipe but with Moorish flavours and makes a beautiful summery meal. The couscous is fragrant with the zests and herbs and the lovely light seafood and broth is a real treat to share with your chums . . . or just make it for yourself. It's nice to use a mixture of fish such as red mullet, gurnard, sea bream or sea bass.

12 large whole prawns
1–2 tbsp olive oil
100ml white wine
750ml fish stock
2 medium tomatoes
3 garlic cloves, crushed
2 tbsp tomato purée
1 red chilli, finely chopped, or
½ tsp chilli flakes
½ tsp cinnamon
750g fish fillets, cut into chunks, skin on
salt and black pepper

Couscous
200g couscous
zest and juice of 1 lemon
zest and juice of 1 clementine (or ½ orange)
¼ tsp ground cinnamon
¼ tsp ground coriander
¼ tsp ground cardamom
½ tsp ground cumin
2 tbsp olive oil
small bunch of parsley
a few mint leaves
small bunch of basil

First make the broth. Remove the heads and shells from the prawns and set them aside. Heat a tablespoon of the oil in a large flameproof casserole dish and add the prawns. Sear them on both sides, then remove them from the pan. Add the prawn heads and shells and cook until they are completely pink. Pour over the wine and allow it to bubble up. Stir vigorously until the bubbles subside and the wine has reduced by half. Pour over the stock, stir to combine it with the wine, then strain it into a jug. Discard the prawn heads and shells .

Skin and finely chop the tomatoes. Add a little more olive oil to the pan and cook the garlic for a couple of minutes, then stir in the tomato purée. Stir until the purée and the oil start to separate, then stir in the tomatoes, chilli or chilli flakes and the cinnamon. Pour over the strained stock, then season with salt and pepper and bring to the boil. Turn down and simmer the broth for 10 minutes, uncovered.

To make the couscous, mix the couscous with the lemon and clementine zest and the spices. Pour over 250ml of the broth and add the citrus juices and olive oil. Cover and leave to stand for about 10 minutes until all the liquid is absorbed. Fluff the couscous up with a fork. Finely chop the parsley and mint and shred the basil, then stir the herbs into the couscous.

Bring the broth back to the boil, then taste and add seasoning if necessary. Add the seared prawns and the fish. Simmer gently for 3–4 minutes at the most, until the fish is just cooked. Serve the couscous in bowls, topped with the fish and prawns, then pour over some broth.

STUFFED SQUID

SERVES 4

The shape of squid cries out for stuffing and we do love a stuffed squid. A medium squid is about 10cm long usually, but they do vary in size so just see what you can get. It doesn't matter if they're bigger and frozen are fine too for this super-charged squid sausage. If you can't find Swiss chard you could use spinach instead.

600g prepared squid
(about 12 medium)

Stuffing
150g Swiss chard
2 tbsp olive oil
1 medium onion,
finely chopped
1 garlic clove
1 tsp fennel seeds
zest of 1 lemon
pinch of chilli flakes
1 medium tomato,
finely chopped
25g pine nuts,
lightly toasted
50g breadcrumbs
1 tbsp finely chopped
flatleaf parsley
2 tbsp finely
chopped basil
salt and black pepper

To serve
100g rocket or similar
salad leaves
lemon wedges

Rinse the squid well inside and out and pat it dry on kitchen paper. Keep the tentacles separate.

Make the stuffing. Separate the chard stems and leaves and finely chop them both. Heat a tablespoon of olive oil in a large frying pan, then add the onion and chard stems and sauté until soft. Add the garlic, fennel seeds, lemon zest and chilli flakes and cook for another minute. Add the tomato and chard leaves, together with 2 tablespoons of water. Season with salt and pepper.

Cook until the tomatoes have broken down and the chard leaves have wilted. The mixture should be fairly dry. Remove the pan from the heat and stir in the pine nuts, breadcrumbs and herbs, then leave to cool. Preheat the oven to 200°C/Fan 180°C/Gas 6.

Stuff the squid, pushing the filling down to the end. Do not overstuff them – leave a centimetre clear at the top and make sure the filling is quite loose, not packed. Fasten the top of each squid with a toothpick to stop the filling from spilling out.

Put the squid in a roasting tin and drizzle them with the remaining olive oil. Add the tentacles and season with salt and pepper. Roast for 15–20 minutes until the squid are opaque and a light golden brown.

Serve the squid on a bed of salad leaves, with some lemon wedges for squeezing over the top.

CELEBRATORY LASAGNE

SERVES 8

*This is our version of Neapolitan lasagne – a fantabulous feast
of meatballs, sausage, tomato sauce, pasta and loads of cheese!
It is amazing. You'll find a recipe for fresh pasta on page 309 if
you want to go the extra mile or you can use bought fresh pasta
or dried lasagne sheets. This is a great dish for a party – nuff said.*

Meatballs

150g minced beef
150g minced pork
50g breadcrumbs
2 garlic cloves, crushed
1 tsp dried sage
1 tsp dried oregano
1 egg
2 tbsp milk
grating of nutmeg
2 tbsp olive oil
salt and black pepper

To assemble

4 large sausages
(preferably Italian style
with fennel seed)
1 quantity of tomato
sauce (see p.310)
½ quantity of fresh pasta
(see p.309), or 18 dried
lasagne sheets
300g ricotta cheese
600g mozzarella
200g Parmesan, grated
bunch of basil,
shredded (reserve a
few whole leaves)

To make the meatballs, put all the ingredients, except the olive oil, in a bowl and season generously with salt and pepper. Mix thoroughly, then form the mixture into small balls of about 20g each – you should get 18–20. Chill the meatballs for 30 minutes. Heat the olive oil in a large saucepan or frying pan (it needs to be big enough to hold the tomato sauce) and brown the meatballs briefly on all sides. Remove the meatballs from the pan.

Skin the sausages and shape them into small rounds about the same size as the meatballs. Fry these on all sides too. Put the meatballs back in the pan and pour over the tomato sauce. Bring to the boil, and leave to simmer for 10 minutes. This helps keep the meatballs and sausage moist during the oven cooking time and also adds flavour to the sauce.

Preheat the oven to 200°C/Fan 180°C/Gas 6. You'll need an oven dish or roasting tin for assembling the lasagne – one about 25 x 35cm is ideal. If using fresh lasagne, roll it out and cut it into 6 sheets – each should be the length of your dish or tin.

Remove the meatballs and sausage from the tomato sauce with a slotted spoon and set them aside. Ladle a quarter of the tomato sauce into the bottom of your dish, then cover with either 2 sheets of fresh pasta or 6 dried sheets. Top with the next quarter of tomato sauce, then cover with half the meatballs and sausage. Take 100g of the ricotta and spoon teaspoons of it over the sauce, in between the meatballs and sausage meat. Sprinkle over 100g of the mozzarella and 50g of the grated Parmesan, followed by some of the basil leaves.

Top with another layer of pasta and repeat, using up another quarter of the tomato sauce, the rest of the meatballs and sausage meat, another 100g each of the ricotta and mozzarella and 50g of the Parmesan. Add more basil.

Finish with the final layer of pasta and cover with the remaining tomato sauce. Top with the rest of the ricotta, mozzarella and Parmesan and add a few basil leaves, tucking them in so they are not completely exposed in the oven.

Bake in the oven for 45–50 minutes, by which time the pasta will be cooked and the top should be brown and bubbling. Remove the lasagne from the oven and leave it to stand for about 10 minutes before cutting. Each serving should stand up well without being sloppy.

CALABRIAN PORK RIBS

SERVES 4

They love their pork in Calabria and this is a favourite way of cooking it. The ribs are bathed in a flavoursome marinade, baked until tender, then finished on the barbecue or grill until charred and fabulous. We used fat end ribs in one piece – basically belly pork on the bone with the skin removed. This is great with some polenta to soak up the juices or with crispy roast potatoes with peppers. The crew demolished this one in just two minutes flat.

rack of pork ribs, in one piece (1.5–2kg)
lemon wedges
salt and black pepper

Marinade
100ml olive oil
2 tbsp red wine vinegar
4 medium-hot red chillies, deseeded and roughly chopped
½ red pepper, roughly chopped
cloves from a bulb of garlic, roughly chopped
a few sprigs of fresh thyme
a few sprigs of fresh rosemary
1 tsp dried oregano
½ tsp chilli flakes

Preheat the oven to 140°C/Fan 120°C/Gas 1. Put all the marinade ingredients into a blender, season with salt and pepper, then blitz until fairly smooth.

Line a roasting tin with foil, making sure there is enough foil hanging over the sides to encase the pork. Place the pork on top of the foil and pour over the marinade. Turn the meat to make sure it is completely covered. Bring the foil together and wrap the pork into a parcel, then put it in the oven. Cook the pork for 2–3 hours, checking it after 2 hours – the meat should be cooked through and tender but nowhere near falling off the bone.

Remove the tin from the oven and put the pork on a chopping board. Pour the cooking juices into a small pan. When the rack is cool enough to handle, cut it into individual ribs – it's easier to follow the bone by turning the rack bone-side up.

Get ready to finish the cooking in one of a few ways – prepare a barbecue, preheat your grill or heat a griddle pan until it is too hot to hold your hand over. Grill or griddle the ribs for about 3–4 minutes on each side until they are well browned and nicely charred in places.

Serve the ribs with lemon wedges, the reheated cooking juices and polenta (see p.308) if you like.

SARDINIA

Sardinia is the second largest island in the Mediterranean, after Sicily, and it is a rugged, mountainous land, with more than 1,100 miles of spectacular coastline. Due to its strategic position in the Med, Sardinia has been colonised by many invaders and in the 14th century was ruled for a while by Catalan conquerors from northern Spain. Their influence still remains and in fact we had our first taste of Catalan food in the town of Alghero on the coast of Sardinia.

Many food traditions are alive and well. With shepherds up in the mountains we ate a kind of black pudding made from sheep's blood stuffed in a sheep's stomach, and we met an old lady of a hundred or more who still did all her own cooking. She made us a minestrone which was her secret for a long life. We also discovered fregola which is made from a wheat dough rubbed into tiny bead-like balls – try our seafood fregola dish on page 70 – and we sampled many different types of Pecorino, the Sardinian cheese made from sheep's milk. Pecorino is used in many dishes including delicious little fried pastries known as seadas, which are served with honey.

We learned how to cook malloreddus, a traditional Sardinian pasta made from semolina flour and flavoured with a little saffron. The dough is formed into little ridged shapes that hold a sauce brilliantly. That one's a keeper for sure.

FRIED CHEESE PASTRIES

WITH HONEY

MAKES 16–18

These are known as seadas in Sardinia and they are amazing, we promise you. We find the dough easier to roll with a pasta machine but you can do it with a rolling pin if you prefer. We cooked something similar in Portugal in 2004 when filming our first television series. They're a Mediterranean classic.

300g ricotta, well drained

1 egg yolk

250g Pecorino cheese, grated

zest of 1 lemon

vegetable oil, for deep-frying

200ml honey, to serve

Pastry

500g plain Italian '00' flour or very fine durum wheat semolina, plus extra for dusting

½ tsp salt

200ml warm water

50g lard or butter, softened

First make the pastry. Put the flour into a bowl with the salt. Gradually stir in the water, then add the lard or butter. Don't worry if the mixture seems very dry at this stage – it will come together as a stiff dough. Wet your hands and knead the dough until it has completely come together, then keep kneading for another 5 minutes until the dough is smooth. Cover the bowl with cling film or a damp tea towel and leave the dough to rest for half an hour.

To make the filling, put the ricotta in a bowl and mix in the egg yolk until well combined. Stir in the Pecorino and lemon zest, then set aside.

Cut the dough into 2 equal pieces and flatten them slightly. Run each piece through a pasta machine on the widest setting, then gradually reduce until the dough is about 2mm thick. Lay each piece out on a lightly floured work surface and cut out 10cm rounds. You should get 16–18. Put a heaped tablespoon of the mixture in the centre of half the rounds, then dampen the edges. Cover with the remaining rounds and seal the edges together with a fork.

To cook, half fill a deep-fat fryer or large saucepan with vegetable oil and heat it to about 160°C. Lower a few pastries into the oil and cook them for 3–4 minutes on each side until golden brown. Don't overcrowd the pan, as this will lower the temperature of the oil. Drain each batch of pastries on kitchen paper. Pour the honey into a small pan and gently warm it through until very runny. Drizzle the honey over the pastries and serve.

SARDINIAN MINESTRONE

SERVES 4-6

The centenarians in Sardinia make their minestrone with loads of lard, but we think this is a nicer version. Minestrone is a much-loved soup all over Italy and it is so good served with this pesto-style dressing. In Sardinia they often use a kind of pasta called fregola in their minestrone, but you could also use broken-up spaghetti or any small pasta if you prefer. If you do have a bit of Parmesan rind in the fridge, sling it into the pot. Even if it looks dry, it'll add flavour.

2 tbsp olive oil

1 onion, finely chopped

1 carrot, finely diced

1 celery stick, finely diced

1 fennel bulb, diced

2 garlic cloves, finely chopped

150g fregola or pasta

400g can of borlotti beans, drained

800ml vegetable or chicken stock or water

2 bay leaves

1 sprig of thyme

1 sprig of rosemary

1 piece of Parmesan cheese rind (optional)

300g broad beans, podded

2 tomatoes, peeled and chopped

½ small green cabbage

150g green beans, trimmed and halved

Heat the oil in a large saucepan. Add the onion, carrot, celery and fennel and cook them gently until softened and starting to colour – this will take 10–15 minutes. Add the garlic and cook for another minute or two, then stir in the fregola and borlotti beans.

Pour over the stock or water and add the herbs and Parmesan rind, if using. Season well with salt and pepper. Bring the soup to the boil, then turn the heat down slightly until it is somewhere between a simmer and a boil and cook for 15 minutes.

Meanwhile, add the broad beans to a small pan of boiling water and blanch them for a minute, then drain. Rinse them in cold water then peel off the skins and set aside.

Add the tomatoes to the soup and cook for another 5 minutes, then add the cabbage, green beans, courgettes and blanched and skinned broad beans. Cover the pan and simmer for a further 5 minutes or until the green vegetables are tender, then add the peas and simmer for another minute or so. Check the seasoning and add more salt and pepper and a squeeze of lemon if you like.

To make the dressing, finely chop the herbs and mix them with the oil – alternatively blitz them together in a blender. Serve the soup with the basil sauce and some grated Parmesan to sprinkle over at the table.

2 courgettes, thinly sliced
into rounds

100g peas (podded
weight, or frozen are fine)

squeeze of lemon
(optional)

salt and black pepper

Dressing

small bunch of basil

few sprigs of parsley

50ml olive oil

25g Parmesan, grated

FOCACCIA

MAKES 1 LOAF

We've done this nice flatbread before and memorably cooked it by the Rialto Bridge in Venice. But as the years go by, we try to make our recipes better and better so give this new version a go. And do you know what? Dave likes to eat focaccia with tuna mayo for breakfast!

500g strong white bread flour

10g instant dried yeast

5g sea salt

pinch of sugar

325ml warm water

2 tbsp olive oil, plus extra for greasing

Topping

50g olives, pitted and halved lengthways (optional)

a few sprigs of rosemary (optional)

2 tbsp olive oil

flaked sea salt

You can make the dough in a stand mixer or by hand. If making it in a mixer, put the flour in the bowl and add the yeast. Stir well before adding the salt and sugar. With the motor running, gradually add the water, followed by the oil. The dough will be fairly wet and sticky to start with. Knead for 5 minutes with the dough hook until you have a smooth, glossy, but still very soft dough.

If you are making the dough by hand, put the dry ingredients in a bowl and add the water and oil gradually until it all comes together. Turn the dough out on to a floured work surface and knead for about 10 minutes.

Leave the dough in a lightly oiled bowl, covered with cling film or a damp tea towel, until it has doubled in size. Oil a roasting tin or brownie tin – it should be at least 30 x 20cm, but slightly larger is fine. Turn out the dough, knock it back and put it in the tin. Using your fingertips, press the dough into the tin, making sure you push it into all the corners. Don't worry if the dough springs back a lot at this stage – it will relax and spread to fill the whole tin. Leave it to rest for 10 minutes, then sprinkle with the olives and rosemary, if using. Drizzle with the olive oil and top with a few flakes of sea salt.

Preheat the oven to 220°C/Fan 200°C/Gas 7. Cover the dough again and leave it to rest for another half an hour until it has risen up again and springs back when you press it. Make indentations in the surface at regular intervals with your fingertip, pressing down to the base of the tin – don't worry, you won't break the dough. Put the bread in the oven and bake for about 20 minutes, until golden brown.

Remove it from the oven and transfer it to a cooling rack. Cover with a cloth again while it cools – this will help keep the crust soft.

MELON SALAD

WITH TOMATOES AND HERBS

SERVES 4

This was Si's idea and it's fresh and fabulous. It's best with a sweet-fleshed orange melon and we've cut everything into differently shaped pieces for contrast and texture. If possible, put this together at the last minute and make sure the tomatoes are at room temperature for the best flavour but the melon and cucumber are well chilled to make the salad refreshing.

½ cucumber
500g melon
4 medium tomatoes
200g fresh, creamy goat's or sheep's cheese
small handful of basil leaves
small handful of mint leaves

Dressing
2 tbsp olive oil
1 tsp white wine vinegar
juice of ½ lemon
salt and black pepper

Peel the cucumber and cut it into slices on the diagonal. Peel the melon and cut it into chunks. Then slice the tomatoes into wedges.

Arrange the cucumber, melon and tomatoes in individual salad bowls or in one big serving dish. Dot over spoonfuls of the cheese, then sprinkle over the basil and mint leaves.

Whisk together the olive oil, vinegar and lemon juice and season with a small pinch of salt and some black pepper. Drizzle the dressing over the salad and serve immediately.

FENNEL AND ORANGE SALAD

SERVES 4

A super-sophisticated salad, this is bursting with flavours that really do seem to capture the atmosphere of the Mediterranean. It's great with oily fish such as mackerel or with pork dishes, and if you're a fan of capers you could add a few to the dressing instead of the mustard. The hazelnuts add a nice bit of crunchy texture.

2 fennel bulbs
3 oranges
25g hazelnuts
small bunch of mint leaves
small bunch of basil leaves
small bunch of fresh oregano leaves (optional)

Dressing
3 tbsp olive oil
juice of ½ lemon
1 tsp red wine vinegar
½ tsp mustard (optional)
salt and black pepper

Trim the base of the fennel bulbs and cut off the stalks. Remove and set aside any feathery fronds. Slice the fennel bulbs lengthways as thinly as you can – the best way to do this is with a mandolin or with a vegetable peeler. Put the slices in a bowl of iced water until you are ready to assemble the salad – they will curl up very attractively.

Prepare the oranges. Top and tail them so they sit upright on your chopping board. Cut the skin away from top to bottom, following the shape of the orange and making sure all the outer membrane is cut away too. Set aside the peel. Slice the oranges thinly, removing any seeds as you do so, then arrange them over a large serving plate or platter.

Put the hazelnuts in a dry frying pan and toast them until they have taken on some colour and are aromatic. Lightly crush them – you want large, non-uniform pieces.

Make the dressing. Put the olive oil, lemon juice, vinegar and mustard, if using, in a large bowl. Squeeze any juice from the orange peelings into the bowl, then season with salt and pepper and whisk thoroughly. Drain the fennel and add it to the dressing. Mix well, then pile everything on top of the orange slices. Sprinkle over the hazelnuts and herbs, including the reserved fennel fronds, and serve at once.

SEAFOOD
WITH SAFFRON FREGOLA
SERVES 4

Fregola is a kind of mini pasta that's very popular in Sardinia. It comes in the shape of beads and looks more like couscous than pasta. This was a great favourite of our director and producer Dick Sharman and it is really good cooking. If you can't get fregola you could use jumbo couscous.

200g mussels, cleaned
200g clams, cleaned
600g shell-on prawns
4 tbsp olive oil
300ml fish stock
500g fregola
1 onion, finely chopped
2 garlic cloves, finely chopped
1 red chilli, finely chopped, or ½ tsp chilli flakes
1 sprig of thyme
1 tsp dried oregano
pinch of saffron, ground
100ml white wine or vermouth
4 medium tomatoes, peeled and roughly chopped
12 small scallops
salt

To serve
small handful of chopped basil and parsley
lemon wedges

Wash the mussels and clams well and discard any with broken shells or any that are open and don't close when given a sharp tap. Take the heads and shells off the prawns and devein them – remove the little black line along the back of each one. Set the prawns and the shells and heads aside.

Heat a tablespoon of the oil in a large, lidded frying pan and add the prawn shells and heads. Fry them for a minute or so until they've turned pink, then pour in the stock. Allow it to bubble up, while stirring vigorously, then leave it to simmer for 5 minutes. Remove the pan from the heat, then strain the stock into a jug and set it aside. Discard the prawn shells and heads.

Bring a large saucepan of water to the boil and add plenty of salt and the fregola. Simmer the fregola for about 10 minutes until it is just al dente, then drain it and set it aside.

While you are cooking the fregola, heat 2 tablespoons of the oil in the frying pan. Add the onion and fry it until softened, then add the garlic, chilli, herbs and saffron. Pour in the wine or vermouth and allow the liquid to reduce for a couple of minutes, then add the reserved stock and the tomatoes. Simmer for 5 minutes, then stir in the cooked fregola. Put the clams and mussels on top, cover the pan and cook for another 2–3 minutes or until the shellfish have opened. Discard any clams and mussels that don't open.

In a separate frying pan heat the remaining olive oil. Sear the prawns on both sides very quickly, then add them to the fregola. Repeat with the scallops. Stir in the basil and parsley and serve immediately with lemon wedges on the side.

MUSSELS ALGHERO

SERVES 4

When you are fed up with moules marinière, try this recipe. It's a Catalan dish we discovered in Alghero, a town on the northwest coast of Sardinia which has historic links to Catalonia. With the rich flavours of anchovy, chilli and tomatoes this is a proper lip smacker!

1kg mussels

2 tbsp olive oil

4 garlic cloves, finely chopped

2 tbsp finely chopped parsley leaves

small bunch of basil, finely chopped

2 anchovy fillets, finely chopped

pinch of chilli flakes

2 medium tomatoes, peeled and finely chopped

150ml white wine

1 tbsp white wine vinegar

salt and black pepper

To serve

thick slices of sour dough or rustic bread

olive oil

Wash the mussels thoroughly. Pull off any beards and discard any mussels that don't close tightly when tapped.

Heat the olive oil in a large saucepan and add the garlic and herbs. Sauté quickly for 2 minutes, then add the anchovy fillets, chilli flakes and tomatoes. Turn down the heat and cook slowly for 5 minutes, then add the wine and white wine vinegar. Season with pepper and taste before you add any salt. Continue to simmer until the sauce has reduced and is creamy orange in colour.

Add the mussels and cook for another 4–5 minutes until all the mussels have opened – discard any that don't. Serve the mussels in big bowls with plenty of the sauce ladled over them and with some thick slices of bread and a bowl of olive oil for dipping.

FRITTO MISTO

SERVES 4 AS A STARTER

Fritto misto – a mixture of fried small fish and shellfish – is on every menu in every Mediterranean fish restaurant. We love it. It's a great dish, best kept simple and just served up with lemon wedges and some bread.

250g squid

250g whitebait or similar small fish

12 large prawns, peeled and heads removed, but tail tips left on

100g plain flour

2 lemons, cut into wedges

mild olive oil, for deep- frying

salt and black pepper

Wash the squid inside and out and make sure it is thoroughly clean. Cut the body into rings and keep the clumps of tentacles whole unless they're very big. Make sure the squid, fish and prawns are very dry.

Put the flour into a shallow bowl and season it with plenty of salt and pepper. Toss the squid, fish and prawns in the plain flour, a few at a time, just before frying.

Half fill a large saucepan or a deep-fat fryer with olive oil. Heat the oil to 180°C or test it by dropping in a small cube of bread – the oil should bubble up furiously around the bread and turn it golden brown.

Pat any excess flour off the squid, fish and prawns and fry them, a few at a time, for about a minute, until light golden brown and crisp. Do not overcrowd the pan, or the temperature of the oil will drop and you will have soggy, oil-laden seafood. Drain each batch on kitchen paper, then wait a minute for the oil to heat up before adding the next batch.

Serve the fried seafood with lemon wedges for squeezing over.

MARINATED SWORDFISH

WITH GREMOLATA

SERVES 4

Gremolata is a savoury topping or relish, made with herbs, olives, capers and lemon – and sometimes breadcrumbs are added. We went fishing off the coast of Sardinia and caught our own swordfish, then cooked this recipe which makes the best of a very special fish. Perfection!

4 swordfish steaks (about 150g each)

200g podded and peeled broad beans (about 1kg fresh unpodded)

1 tbsp olive oil

100ml white wine

20g butter

salt and black pepper

Marinade

50ml olive oil

zest and juice of 1 lemon

2 garlic cloves, crushed

1 tsp dried oregano

Gremolata

pared zest of 1 lemon, finely chopped

50g green olives, pitted and finely chopped

50g capers, finely chopped

25g flatleaf parsley, finely chopped

Season the swordfish steaks with salt and black pepper and put them in a bowl. Mix all the ingredients for the marinade together and pour it over the swordfish. Leave the fish to marinate for no longer than 15 minutes – you don't want the lemon to 'cook' the fish.

While the swordfish is marinating, prepare everything else. Blanch the broad beans in boiling water for 2 minutes, then drain them and set them aside. Make the gremolata by mixing together the pared lemon zest, olives, capers and parsley.

Heat the tablespoon of olive oil in a heavy-based frying pan. When the pan is very hot, add the swordfish steaks and sear them for 3–4 minutes on each side. Remove them from the pan and set them aside to rest while you finish the sauce. Deglaze the pan with the white wine, then add the butter. Swirl until the butter has melted, then add the blanched broad beans and heat them through.

Serve the swordfish with the sauce spooned over and the gremolata on the side.

SEARED FISH
WITH FENNEL RISOTTO
SERVES 4

With its rosy pink skin, red mullet is a beautiful-looking fish and it's also delicious to eat. If you can't find red mullet, you can use any fairly thin fish fillets with skin that crisps up well when cooked. Bream or sea bass are both good. This is our idea of great food.

1 tsp olive oil
4 x 100–150g fillets of red mullet
salt and black pepper

Fennel risotto

1.2 litres chicken or vegetable stock
2 tbsp olive oil
30g butter
1 large onion, finely chopped
1 large fennel bulb, finely chopped (reserve leafy fronds)
2 garlic cloves, finely chopped
zest of 1 lemon, finely grated
300g risotto rice
100ml white wine or vermouth
25g Parmesan, grated
squeeze of lemon juice (optional)
a few basil leaves

First make the risotto. Pour the stock into a saucepan and bring it to simmering point. Heat the olive oil with half the butter in a separate large pan. When the butter has melted and started to foam, add the onion and fennel and cook slowly over a gentle heat until soft and translucent. Add the garlic, lemon zest and the rice. Stir until the rice is glossy.

Turn up the heat and pour in the wine or vermouth. Leave it to bubble up for a minute until most of it has boiled off, then turn down the heat to medium. Add a ladleful of the hot stock and stir continuously until it has all been absorbed. Repeat until you have added all the stock – by this time the rice should be creamy and cooked but still have a little bite to it.

Add the rest of the butter and Parmesan and beat vigorously. Taste and add a squeeze of lemon juice if necessary. Garnish with few basil leaves and any feathery fronds from the fennel.

To cook the fish, take a large, flat-bottomed frying pan. Drizzle the pan very lightly with olive oil, then heat until it is almost too hot to hold your hand over for more than 2–3 seconds. Season the fish fillets with salt and pepper and carefully score the skin in a few places if you like. Place the fillets skin-side down in the frying pan and press flat with the back of a spatula. Lower the heat to medium. After 3–4 minutes, when you can see that the fish is turning opaque up the sides and the edges are crisp and brown, try to flip it. If it has cooked enough it should easily lift from the pan, but leave it for a little longer if it doesn't want to come away. When you have turned the fillets over, sear the top side for a minute. Serve the fish, skin-side up, on top of the risotto.

LINGUINE WITH TUNA

SERVES 4

Andreas, a tuna chef in the town of Carloforte, made this epic dish for us and it was the first thing we wanted to cook when we got home to the UK. It's just an assembly job but it's perfect and a great store-cupboard supper – simple, quick and tasty. He had fresh tuna, of course, but we use tuna in oil from a can or jar for this recipe.

400g linguine

150–200g canned or jarred tuna (drained weight)

50g capers

50g green pitted olives, sliced

zest of 1 lemon

2 tbsp grated Parmesan

2 tbsp finely chopped flatleaf parsley

pinch of chilli flakes (optional)

1 tbsp olive oil

salt and black pepper

To serve

1 tbsp finely chopped parsley

1–2 tbsp grated Parmesan

Bring a large saucepan of water to the boil and add salt. Add the pasta and cook it until al dente.

While the pasta is cooking, put the tuna in a large bowl and gently break it into flakes. Add the capers, olives, lemon zest, Parmesan, parsley and chilli flakes, if using. Stir lightly to combine.

Reserve a ladleful of the pasta cooking liquid, then drain the pasta. Add the pasta to the bowl and drizzle over the olive oil. Add about 100ml of the cooking liquid and mix until the strands of linguine separate and are coated in the sauce.

Season with salt and pepper, then serve immediately, sprinkled with the extra parsley and cheese.

CACIO E PEPE

PASTA WITH CHEESE AND BLACK PEPPER

SERVES 4

We had to sneak this one in, even though it's really more Roman than Mediterranean. Dave ate it in a restaurant in Rome earlier this year and went bonkers for it. Tonnarelli (a square-cut spaghetti) is traditionally used for this dish in Rome, but elsewhere it's made with regular spaghetti. You use less water than usual to cook the pasta so the starches released are more concentrated, ideal for the sauce. It's like a purist macaroni cheese. Remember to go heavy on the pepper and if you fancy, finish it all off with a dash of olive oil.

1 tbsp black peppercorns
400g spaghetti or tonnarelli
150g Pecorino cheese, grated
olive oil (optional)
salt

Lightly toast the peppercorns in a dry frying pan until you can smell their lovely aroma, then grind them to a coarse texture, preferably using a pestle and mortar. Set them aside.

Half fill a large saucepan with water and bring it to the boil. Add salt and the pasta – the water should just cover the pasta when it has fully submerged – and cook until the pasta is al dente. Stir every so often to make sure the pasta isn't sticking to the base of the pan.

Ladle off about 500ml of the cooking water, then drain the pasta. Put the peppercorns and cheese in a large bowl and whisk in some of the reserved cooking liquid, a little at a time, until you have a paste. Continue adding liquid until the mixture is the consistency of a thin béchamel sauce.

Add the pasta and toss everything well. If the pasta clumps together, continue adding the pasta cooking liquid until the strands separate easily and are individually coated with the sauce. Serve immediately with a little more ground pepper and a dash of olive oil if you like.

PASTA

WITH FRESH TOMATOES AND PECORINO

SERVES 4

Pecorino is a sheep's milk cheese and it's everywhere in Sardinia. There are so many varieties – sardo, romano and dolce to name but a few. We all know that sometimes simplest is best, and when a dish is done with really good ingredients it doesn't come much better than this. With barely any cooking, this is a perfect showcase for good Pecorino.

600g fresh very ripe tomatoes

2 tbsp olive oil

2 garlic cloves, crushed

sprig of oregano, left whole

400g spaghetti or linguine

salt and black pepper

To serve

a few basil leaves, shredded

a good hunk of Pecorino sardo cheese, shaved

First prepare the tomatoes. Bring a kettle of water to the boil. Score a cross on the base of each tomato, then put them in a bowl and pour over the freshly boiled water. Count to 10, then check the tomatoes. If they are very ripe, the skin should easily break when you insert a knife. If they are less ripe, they may need to stand for slightly longer. When you think the tomatoes are ready to peel, pour off the water. Leave them until cool enough to handle and the skins should slip off easily.

Slice the tomatoes in half, then cut out their green cores and scoop out the seeds into a sieve over a bowl. Finely chop the tomato flesh.

To make the sauce, heat the oil in a frying pan. Add the garlic and cook it for 2–3 minutes. Add the tomato flesh and fry it over a high heat for another 2–3 minutes, then pour in the reserved juice from the seeds. Season with salt and pepper and add the oregano sprig. Bring to the boil and simmer the tomatoes for about 10 minutes – they will give out liquid and start reducing down. When most of the liquid has reduced, your sauce is ready.

Meanwhile, bring a large saucepan of water to the boil and add a generous amount of salt. Cook the pasta until just al dente, then drain. Immediately add the pasta to the sauce and toss so it is well coated.

Serve the pasta in shallow bowls with a garnish of basil leaves and plenty of shavings of cheese.

MALLOREDDUS

SARDINIAN GNOCCHI

SERVES 4

This maggot-shaped, gnocchi-like pasta is made from fine semolina instead of flour and is a great Sardinian speciality. We learned how to make our own and serve it with a punchy sausage, white wine and tomato sauce and lots of Sardinian Pecorino cheese. Traditionally the malloreddus are shaped on a special piece of kit – a gnocchi ridger – to form little grooves that catch and hold the delicious sauce. If you don't have a ridger, you can shape them on the tines of a fork.

Malloreddus

300g fine semolina, plus extra for dusting

large pinch of saffron threads

160ml just-boiled water

sea salt

Sauce

1 tbsp olive oil

1 onion, finely chopped

4 Italian sausages, skinned

pinch of saffron threads

1 tsp oregano

1 tbsp tomato purée

100ml white wine

4 ripe tomatoes, peeled and chopped

To serve

a few basil leaves, torn

Parmesan or Pecorino cheese, grated

To make the malloreddus, put the semolina in a bowl. Grind the saffron with a generous pinch of sea salt using a pestle and mortar. Add this to the semolina. Gradually work in the water until you have a dough that forms a ball. Turn the dough out on to a lightly floured work surface and knead until smooth. The dough should be elastic and not sticky. Alternatively, make the dough in a stand mixer and knead it with the dough hook for 5 minutes. Wrap the dough in cling film and leave it to rest for about an hour.

Cut the dough into 4 even pieces, then roll each piece into a sausage shape, about 1cm in diameter. Cut the rolls into 3cm lengths.

To shape the malloreddus, use a gnocchi ridger. Dust it generously with more semolina and place a piece of the dough towards the top of the ridger. Using your 3 middle fingers, firmly roll the dough down the ridger to make a ridged piece of dough that curls round on itself. Put the malloreddus on a floured surface and continue until you have used all the dough. Set the malloreddus aside while you make the sauce.

To make the sauce, heat the olive oil in a saucepan. Add the onion and sauté it for about 10 minutes until soft and translucent. Add the sausage meat and break it up into small pieces with a spoon. Sear it on the underside, then turn it all over and continue until it is lightly browned.

Grind the saffron threads with a pinch of sea salt using a pestle and mortar. Sprinkle this over the sausage along with the oregano, then stir in the tomato purée. Stir to combine and allow the tomato purée to cook out a little, then pour in the wine. Add the tomatoes and bring to the boil. Reduce the heat and leave to simmer, uncovered, for about half an hour until well reduced, stirring the sauce regularly to make sure it doesn't catch on the bottom. If it is getting a little dry, add a splash of water.

Bring a large saucepan of water to the boil and add salt. Add the malloreddus and cook them for 3–4 minutes, or until they have risen to the top. Remove them with a slotted spoon and add them to the sauce, along with a small ladleful of the pasta cooking liquid. Stir gently to combine, then sprinkle with basil leaves and serve with grated cheese.

CHICKEN

WITH CAPERS

SERVES 4

Capers are a big thing in Sardinian cooking and we love their flavour. This chicken dish is so simple to make and with olive oil, lemon and basil it's packed with Mediterranean flavours. This is great served with the Sardinian pasta malloreddus (see pages 82–83).

2 tbsp olive oil

4 chicken legs or 8 chicken thighs, skin on, bone in

1 onion, finely sliced

2 garlic cloves, finely chopped

200ml white wine

3 tbsp capers in brine, drained and rinsed

zest of 1 lemon

small bunch of basil leaves, finely chopped

small bunch of flat leaf parsley leaves, finely chopped

salt and black pepper

Heat the olive oil in a large heavy-based frying pan or a flameproof casserole dish. Season the chicken with salt and pepper, then fry it, skin-side down, over a medium to high heat until well browned. This will take longer than you think – probably about 10 minutes. Turn the chicken over and fry it on the underside for another 5 minutes.

Remove the chicken from the pan and add the onion. Fry it over a low to medium heat, stirring regularly, until it's starting to soften. Add the garlic and cook for another couple of minutes. Add the white wine, capers and lemon zest, then place the chicken pieces on top.

Partially cover the pan and cook for about 10 minutes until the chicken is completely cooked through – if you pierce the thickest part of the thigh, the juices should run clear. If it looks as though it is getting a little dry, add a splash of water.

To serve, remove the chicken from the pan and put it on a warm serving platter. Add the basil and parsley to the pan and stir just until they wilt down, then spoon the juices over the chicken.

SARDINIAN LAMB

WITH FENNEL

SERVES 4

This is one of the best lamb stews we've ever cooked. Lamb and fennel is a very popular combination in Sardinia and makes a wonderfully fragrant dish. Serve this with couscous or hunks of good bread, or add some new potatoes to the casserole.

1kg lamb neck fillet or shoulder

1 tbsp flour

1 tbsp fennel seeds, ground

pinch of ground saffron

4 tbsp olive oil

1 large onion, finely chopped

4 garlic cloves, finely chopped

½–1 tsp chilli flakes

2 pieces of pared orange zest

300ml white wine

up to 300ml lamb stock

2 large tomatoes, peeled and diced

bouquet garni (2 bay leaves, a sprig of parsley, a sprig of rosemary)

2 fennel bulbs

squeeze of lemon juice (optional)

Cut the lamb into 6cm chunks and put it in a bowl. Season it with salt and pepper. Sprinkle over the flour, fennel seeds and saffron and turn the lamb to make sure all the pieces are coated. Heat a tablespoon of the oil in a large flameproof casserole dish. Sear the lamb on all sides, making sure you get a good, deep brown crust all over. Do this in a few batches – if you crowd the pan too much the lamb won't brown properly. Set each batch aside as it is browned.

Add a little more of the oil to the casserole dish if necessary, turn down the heat and fry the onion until it's soft and translucent. Add the garlic and cook for a further minute or so, then add the chilli flakes and pared zest. Turn up the heat, pour in the wine and stir, scraping up any brown bits from the base of the pan.

Put the lamb back in the casserole dish, then pour in enough of the stock to just cover the lamb. Add the tomatoes and the bouquet garni. Bring to the boil, then turn down the heat to a low simmer. Put a lid on the dish and cook for an hour.

Meanwhile, prepare the fennel. Trim the top, cutting off any fronds and saving them for later. Trim as little as possible from the base of the fennel, then cut the bulb in half, lengthways. Cut each half into 3 wedges, also lengthways. These should hold together, although the outer layers may come away from the root. Heat the remaining olive oil in a large frying pan, then sear the pieces of fennel until they have caramelised round the edges. Set aside.

small bunch of parsley,
finely chopped
small bunch of basil,
shredded
salt and black pepper

When the lamb has cooked for an hour, add the fennel. Continue to cook, uncovered, for a further 20 minutes, until the fennel is very tender and the liquid has reduced down a little. Taste for seasoning, and add more salt, pepper and a squeeze of lemon juice if necessary.

Remove the lemon zest and the bouquet garni. Stir in the parsley and basil and leave the dish to stand off the heat for a couple of minutes. Finely chop any reserved fennel fronds and sprinkle them over the casserole. Serve in large, shallow bowls.

PORK ESCALOPES

WITH SALSA VERDE

SERVES 4

Well pickle my pork! Who said salsa verde was only good with fish?
It is so, so tasty served with this sage-seasoned pork and this makes
a simple, yet very special supper.

4 slices of pork loin
1 tbsp flour
½ tsp dried sage
1 tbsp olive oil
15g butter
salt and black pepper

Salsa verde

2 garlic cloves, finely chopped
1 tsp red wine vinegar
1 tbsp lemon juice
4 anchovy fillets
small bunch of flatleaf parsley, leaves only
small bunch of basil, leaves only
125ml olive oil
50g capers, drained, rinsed and roughly chopped

First make the salsa verde. Put the garlic, vinegar, lemon juice, anchovy fillets and herbs in a food processor. Drizzle in the oil while the motor is running, then add the roughly chopped capers. The texture can be as smooth or as coarse as you like. Taste to check the seasoning and add a little salt if needed.

Place a slice of pork between 2 sheets of cling film and bash it with a rolling pin or a meat mallet until it is about ½ cm thick all over. Remove the cling film, set the pork aside and repeat with the remaining slices. Mix the flour and sage together and season with salt and pepper. Dust the pork with this mixture, patting off any excess.

Heat the olive oil and butter in a large frying pan. When the butter has melted and started to foam, add a couple of the pork escalopes and cook them for 2–3 minutes on each side until crisp and brown. Remove them from the pan and keep them warm while you cook the rest.

Serve the pork with the salsa verde on the side to spoon over the top.

CORSICA

We weren't sure whether Corsica would seem French or Italian and it turns out it's neither – it's Corsican with its own very special identity. It is a beautiful mountainous island and the smell of the wild herbs, known as maquis, covering the land follows you everywhere you go. François Gandolfi, our friend and series director/producer, has Corsica running through his veins and this was his chance to show off the island he knows and loves.

We spent our first night in Corsica in the town of Bonifacio on the southern tip of the island, where we feasted on stuffed mussels. They were so good we had to get the recipe to include here. We also ate the best veal we'd ever tasted in Corsica. It came from a Corsican breed of cow known as tiger cows – because they're stripy! They roam free on the hillsides, feeding on the wild herbs which give their meat a special flavour. We sampled some with the farmer and his brother, who is a chef, and it was sensationally good. Fortunately this recipe is also excellent with some British rose veal.

They like their meat in Corsica and pork is hugely important. There's a wide range of salamis, sausages and other pork products. We've adapted a local dish that we particularly enjoyed – lentils with a special sausage called figatelli – to make with Italian fennel sausages and it works brilliantly. We've also got a great recipe for wild boar – again, something that's popular in Corsica – but you can also make it with pork if you're all out of wild boar.

FRIED GOAT'S CHEESE

SERVES 4 AS A STARTER

Those little logs of goat's cheese with a rind and a slightly oozy, chalky texture are just right here for these delicious little morsels. The hint of garlic in the frying oil adds extra flavour, and the chilli salsa is the perfect accompaniment – an indulgent veggie treat fit for the gods.

500g goat's cheese
50g plain flour
2 eggs
75g breadcrumbs
(fresh or panko)
2 tsp herbes de Provence
olive oil, for frying
2 garlic cloves, sliced
salt and black pepper

Salsa (optional)
1 tbsp olive oil
1 tbsp red wine vinegar
½ tsp honey
4 tomatoes, finely diced
½ red onion, finely chopped
1 small garlic clove,
finely chopped
1 red chilli, finely chopped
or ½ tsp chilli flakes
1 sprig rosemary, leaves
only, very finely chopped
handful of flatleaf parsley
leaves, chopped
handful of basil leaves,
shredded

OR
2 tbsp honey

If using the salsa, make that first so you can leave the flavours to develop while you cook the cheese. Put the olive oil, vinegar and honey in a bowl and stir until the honey has dissolved. Add the remaining ingredients and season with salt and pepper. Set aside.

Cut the rind off the cheese and slice it into rounds. Spread the flour on a small plate. Crack one of the eggs into a small bowl and beat it. Put half the breadcrumbs on a small plate, add half the herbs and stir to combine. Season with salt and pepper.

Dip a slice of cheese in the flour and dust off any excess. Dip it in the egg, again shaking off any excess, then press it into the breadcrumbs and turn it over until the cheese is completely coated. Set aside and continue until you've coated half the cheese. Then add the remaining egg to the bowl and put the rest of the breadcrumbs on the plate, getting rid of the first batch if it is particularly messy.

When you have coated all the cheese, cover the base of a large frying pan with olive oil – it should be about 1cm deep. Add the garlic and fry until it just starts to colour, then remove it immediately. Fry the cheese in batches – don't overcrowd the pan or the cheese will not crisp up – and drain them on kitchen paper.

Serve the fried cheese with the salsa or with gently warmed honey.

STUFFED ONIONS

SERVES 4 AS A LIGHT SUPPER OR 8 AS A SIDE DISH OR STARTER

Cheese and onion is a winner in anybody's language and this recipe gives the humble allium the respect it deserves. The stuffing is enhanced with lots of fresh herbs and you can add 75 grams of tasty air-dried ham to the stuffing too if you like.

8 medium onions
(150–250g each)

200g ricotta or brocciu
(Corsican sheep's cheese)

50g Pecorino or similar
hard cheese, grated

1 egg, beaten

1 garlic clove, crushed

small bunch of flatleaf
parsley, finely chopped

small bunch of mint,
finely chopped

few sprigs of thyme,
finely chopped

2 sprigs of tarragon,
finely chopped

2 tbsp olive oil

100ml white wine

salt and black pepper

Peel the onions, leaving as much of the root base and stem intact as you can, but making sure you've trimmed off any brown skin. Bring a large saucepan of water to the boil. When it is bubbling fiercely, add some salt and the onions. Bring the water back to the boil, partially cover the pan, and cook the onions for 10 minutes. They will still be firm, but the outer layer will have softened slightly and will give a little when you press it. Remove the onions from the saucepan and leave them to cool.

To make the filling, put the cheeses, egg, garlic and herbs in a bowl and season with salt and pepper, then mix thoroughly. Preheat the oven to 180°C/Fan 160°C/Gas 4.

Cut off the top third off each onion and set the tops aside. Pull out the inner layers of the onions, leaving just 3 or 4 outer layers – you can use the inner bits in another recipe. If you notice holes at the bottom of your onions, use some of the layers you've taken out to patch them up. Spoon the filling into the onions, then replace their tops.

Drizzle a little of the olive oil into an ovenproof dish that's large enough to hold the onions snuggly – they shouldn't have much space around them. Pour over the wine along with 100ml of water and the remaining oil and season with salt and pepper. Cover the dish with foil.

Bake the onions in the preheated oven for 20 minutes. Then remove the foil and bake for another 40–45 minutes until the onions are tender and the outer layers are slightly caramelised in places. Serve the onions with the juices from the dish spooned over the top.

STORZAPRETTI

CORSICAN DUMPLINGS

MAKES ABOUT 20 – ENOUGH FOR 4

This traditional Corsican recipe is basically little savoury dumplings baked in a tasty tomato sauce. It makes a wonderfully robust veggie supper if you're okay with the cheese. The dumplings are egg-shaped – the posh name for them is quenelles – and they are quite easy to shape with a couple of spoons so give this a go.

300g ricotta
500g Swiss chard
50g fine breadcrumbs
1 egg, beaten
1 tbsp finely chopped basil
1 tbsp finely chopped mint
50g Pecorino cheese, grated
fine semolina or '00' flour, for dusting
salt and black pepper

Corsican tomato sauce

3 red peppers
2 tbsp olive oil
1 onion, finely chopped
2 garlic cloves, chopped
1 bay leaf
1 sprig thyme
1 sprig rosemary
150ml red wine
400g can tomatoes or 8 medium tomatoes, peeled

To finish

50g Gruyère cheese, grated
50g Pecorino cheese or brocciu, grated

Drain the ricotta in a sieve to get rid of any excess liquid and put it in a bowl. Remove the white ribs from the chard and set them aside to use another time. Wash the leaves thoroughly, chop them roughly and put them in a saucepan with a little water and a pinch of salt. Bring the water to the boil, then simmer until the leaves have wilted down and are softened. Run the chard under cold water until it's cool, then squeeze out as much liquid as possible. Chop the chard as finely as you can.

Add the chard to the ricotta together with the breadcrumbs, egg, herbs and cheese. Mix well, then leave the mixture to chill in the fridge for about an hour until it has firmed up a little. Lightly dust a baking tray with the fine semolina. Take 2 dessertspoons and use them to form little egg-shaped dumplings (quenelles) from the mixture, scraping it from one spoon to the other until you have a neat shape. Drop the dumpling on to the baking tray and keep going until you have used up all the mixture – you should get about 20 dumplings.

Bring a large saucepan of water to the boil and add a generous amount of salt. Sprinkle the dumplings with semolina or flour so they are coated and pat off any excess. Cook the dumplings in 2 batches. When they float to the top they will be ready – this should take 3–4 minutes.

To make the sauce, preheat the oven to 200°C/Fan 180°C/Gas 6. Cut the peppers in half and place them on a baking tray. Roast in the preheated oven until the skin has started to blacken – about 25 minutes. Remove the peppers from the oven, put them in a bowl and cover. When they are cool enough to handle, peel off the skin and finely chop the flesh.

Heat the olive oil in a saucepan and add the onion. Sauté over a low to medium heat for about 10 minutes, until soft, then add the peppers and garlic and cook for a further 5 minutes. Add the herbs and the wine. Bring to the boil, allow the wine to reduce by half, then add the tomatoes. Return to the boil, then lower the heat to a gentle simmer and leave to cook, uncovered, for about 10 minutes until the sauce has slightly thickened. Discard the herbs.

Lightly oil an ovenproof dish and add half the sauce. Put the cooked dumplings on top and cover with the remaining sauce. Sprinkle with the cheese and bake in the oven for about 20 minutes, until lightly browned.

LENTILS WITH SAUSAGE

SERVES 6

They like their lentils in Corsica and a great way of serving them is with a traditional liver sausage called figatelli, beloved by locals but almost impossible to find elsewhere. It's a simple dish – strong and direct, a bit like the Corsicans themselves – and we think it works well with Cumberland or Italian fennel sausages too.

1 tbsp olive oil

8 Italian-style sausages

2 red onions, sliced into wedges

2 large carrots, sliced into rounds

3 garlic cloves, finely chopped

300g lentils, well rinsed

1 litre vegetable or chicken stock or water

2 bay leaves

1 sprig of thyme

1 sprig of sage

1 sprig of tarragon

4 medium tomatoes, peeled and finely chopped

100g leafy greens (spring greens, kale, chard, cavolo nero), shredded

salt and black pepper

Heat the oil in a large flameproof casserole dish. Add the sausages and sear until they're nice and brown on all sides. Remove them from the dish. Add the onions and carrots and cook them over a high heat for 5 minutes until slightly browned. Add the garlic and cook for a further minute, then stir in the lentils.

Pour over the stock or water and season with salt and pepper. Bring to the boil and cook briskly for 10 minutes, partially covered. By the end of this cooking time, the lentils should just be starting to give a little if you squeeze them. Add the herbs and tomatoes and return the sausages to the pan. Turn down the heat slightly to a simmer and continue to cook, uncovered, for a further 20 minutes until the lentils are just cooked through and the vegetables are tender. Check the liquid level in the pan – the texture shouldn't be soupy, but you need enough liquid for the lentils not to catch on the bottom.

Bring a saucepan of water to the boil and add salt. Add the greens and cook them for a few minutes until they have wilted down. Drain and stir the greens through the lentils, then tip everything into a serving dish or ladle into shallow bowls.

CORSICAN HERB SOUP

SERVES 4

This sounds quite plain but it's really a Cinderella story – something simple transformed into a thing of beauty. The herb dressing and cheesy topping makes this simple bowlful of Mediterranean veg something special. If you like, you could add spoonfuls of thick Greek yoghurt instead of the cheese.

2 tbsp olive oil

1 large onion, finely chopped

2 garlic cloves, finely chopped

500g Swiss chard, leaves only

200g spinach

small bunch of parsley

a few sprigs of tarragon, leaves only

1 tbsp dried mint

1 litre hot vegetable stock or water

salt and black pepper

To serve

1 tbsp olive oil

1 tbsp lemon juice

2 tbsp chopped flatleaf parsley leaves

a few sprigs of tarragon

a few mint leaves

a few basil leaves, plus extra to garnish

100g ricotta or brocciu (Corsican sheep's cheese)

Heat the olive oil in a large saucepan. Add the onion and sauté it gently for at least 10 minutes until it's very soft and translucent. Add the garlic and continue to cook for a couple of minutes.

Wash the chard and spinach leaves well, then shred them finely. Add them to the pan, pressing them down so they wilt quickly, then add the parsley, tarragon and mint. Stir to combine, then pour over the hot stock or water. Season with salt and black pepper.

Bring the soup to the boil, then turn the heat down and simmer for 5 minutes. Check for seasoning, then blitz until smooth in a blender or using a stick blender.

Put the olive oil, lemon juice and herbs in a food processor and blend to make a lovely bright green oil. Ladle the hot soup into bowls, add a spoonful of the ricotta or brocciu to each serving, then drizzle with the herby dressing. Garnish with fresh basil leaves.

KIDNEY BEAN AND HAM HOCK STEW

SERVES 6–8

We ate soupy stews like this one in Corsica – they love their pig there – and those inspired us to write this recipe. It's like a super-special version of the classic split pea and ham soup that we love at home – full of greens and really rustic and hearty. As our mothers used to say, 'Eat this and you'll live forever!' Just don't forget to soak your beans.

1 small ham hock, unsmoked

250g dried red kidney beans, soaked overnight

2 onions

3 large carrots

3 celery sticks

2 bay leaves

1 sprig each of thyme, oregano, parsley and tarragon

2 large potatoes, cut into chunks

3 leeks, sliced

2 medium tomatoes, peeled and diced

200g Swiss chard leaves, shredded

1 large courgette, cut into rounds

salt and black pepper

To serve

tarragon, mint and parsley leaves, finely chopped

Put the ham hock in a large saucepan and cover it with water. Bring the water to the boil and after 2 minutes, take the pan off the heat and drain off the water. Rinse the saucepan and the ham hock under cold water to get rid of the white starch, then put the hock back in the saucepan. Add the soaked and drained kidney beans and just cover with fresh water. Bring the water to the boil and boil hard for 10 minutes, skimming off any foam from the surface.

Cut the onions into wedges and the carrots and celery into chunks, then add them to the pan with the bay leaves and sprigs of herbs. Simmer quite briskly for an hour. By this time the kidney beans should be cooked but still have a little bite. Remove the ham hock from the saucepan and when it is cool enough to handle, remove the skin, fat and bone and pull the meat into small chunks. Put the meat in the pan.

Add the potatoes and leeks. Continue to cook for half an hour, then add the tomatoes, chard and courgette and cook for another half an hour. The potatoes should have broken up into the broth and thickened it slightly and the vegetables should be very tender.

To serve, stir in the chopped herbs, then remove the pan from the heat and leave the soup to stand for a few minutes before ladling it into bowls.

BEAN CASSEROLE

SERVES 4

Beanz meanz yummy – this could be a meal in itself but is also a very good accompaniment to lamb. Pulses play a huge part in the Mediterranean way of eating and they are really tasty and good for you too. We like to make this with flageolet beans, a type of haricot bean with a lovely light green colour. To make this extra special, serve with the herb oil on page 311.

250g dried flageolet beans
2 bay leaves
2 sprigs of rosemary
1 tsp salt
1 bulb of garlic

Casserole
1 tbsp olive oil
15g butter
1 onion, finely chopped
2 celery sticks, finely chopped
2 leeks, sliced into rounds
2 large carrots, diced
150g celeriac, diced (optional)
3 garlic cloves, finely chopped
200ml white wine
sprig of rosemary, leaves finely chopped
sprig of thyme, leaves finely chopped
4 medium tomatoes, peeled and chopped (or 400g can of tomatoes)
salt and black pepper

Soak the beans overnight before cooking. When you are ready to cook them, rinse them thoroughly and put them in a large saucepan with the bay, rosemary and salt. Cut the garlic in half horizontally and add it to the pan. Cover with water and bring to the boil, then turn the heat down slightly and continue to cook for 1–1½ hours. Check regularly to make sure there's enough water and the beans aren't becoming mushy – you want them just cooked, so very slightly al dente.

For the casserole, heat the olive oil and butter in a large saucepan. Add the onion, celery, leeks, carrots and celeriac, if using. Fry the vegetables gently over a medium heat for 10–15 minutes, until they have started to soften and brown around the edges. Add the garlic and cook for a couple of minutes longer, then pour in the white wine. Bring the wine to the boil and let most of it evaporate, then add the herbs and tomatoes. Add the beans and just enough water to cover them. Season generously with salt and pepper.

Bring to the boil, then reduce the temperature and put a lid on the pan. Simmer for 30–45 minutes until the vegetables are very tender. The texture of the dish should be slightly loose – you shouldn't be able to stand your spoon up in it. Check the seasoning and serve with the herb oil (see p.311) to drizzle over the beans.

HERB AND CHARD TART

SERVES 4

Si loves a gutsy rustic tart like this one! Brocciu is a Corsican soft sheep's milk cheese, which is great in this, but if you can't find any, use ricotta instead. The Pecorino adds intensity to the flavour. Chard is hugely popular in Corsica and we love it too. We've made this with shortcrust pastry but you can also use puff if you fancy.

200g chard
1 tbsp olive oil
15g butter
1 leek, finely sliced into rounds
pinch of salt
squeeze of lemon juice, plus grated zest
2 garlic cloves, finely chopped
1 tsp dried sage
1 tsp dried oregano
small bunch of flatleaf parsley, roughly chopped
small bunch of mint, leaves only, roughly chopped
50g Pecorino, grated
100g brocciu or ricotta cheese
1 egg, beaten

Pastry
200g plain flour
pinch of salt
60g chilled butter, cut into cubes
60g lard
1–2 tbsp iced water

First make the pastry. Put the flour in a bowl and add a generous pinch of salt. Add the butter and lard and rub them in with your fingers, until the mixture resembles fine breadcrumbs. Work in just enough of the iced water to bind the dough together – the less water, the shorter your pastry. Alternatively, make this in a food processor or stand mixer. Roll the dough into a ball and wrap it in cling film. Chill it in the fridge for at least half an hour while you make the filling.

Separate the leaves and stems of the chard and shred them. Heat the oil and butter in a large frying pan. Add the leek and the chard stems, along with a pinch of salt and a squeeze of lemon. Cover and braise the veg in the buttery juices until softened. Add the chard leaves, lemon zest, garlic and dried herbs. Continue to cook, stirring regularly, until the chard has wilted down. Remove from the heat and stir in the fresh herbs and the Pecorino. Leave to cool.

Preheat the oven to 200°C/Fan 180°C/Gas 6. Lightly flour a work surface and roll the pastry out into a large circle about 30cm in diameter. Don't worry if it is a bit ragged around the edges. Transfer the pastry to a baking tray, then spread the filling over the centre of the pastry, making sure you leave a border of at least 3–4cm. Dot dessertspoons of the brocciu or ricotta over the top. Bring the edges of the pastry up over the filling – you will find that a large part of it will be exposed, but this is how it should be. Pleat the edges lightly, then brush with beaten egg.

Bake the tart in the oven for about 30 minutes or until the pastry and any exposed cheese is a light golden brown. Leave to cool slightly before serving.

COURGETTE GRATIN

SERVES 4 AS A SIDE DISH

This is a great dish to make when courgettes are in season and cheap. It transforms the humble courgette into a rich treat of a side dish, which is great with meat or with a tomato salad as a veggie main. Adding the flour to the crème fraiche and milk is a top tip, as it stops them from curdling.

2 tbsp olive oil
800g courgettes, sliced into ½cm rounds
a few sprigs of thyme
a few basil leaves
100ml crème fraiche
50ml milk
1 tsp flour
75g Gruyère cheese or similar, grated
salt and black pepper

Preheat the oven to 200°C/Fan 180°C/Gas 6.

Heat the olive oil in a large frying pan that has a lid. Add the courgettes and herbs and season with salt and pepper. Cover the pan and cook the courgettes gently for up to 10 minutes, stirring every so often, until they have softened slightly but are still al dente. The oil will take on a deep, rich green colour from the courgettes.

Tip everything into an ovenproof dish. Whisk the crème fraiche, milk and flour together and season with salt. Pour this mixture over the courgettes. It will not be enough to cover them completely, but this is fine – it will bubble up when cooking.

Sprinkle the cheese on top and bake the gratin in the oven for about 25 minutes until it's brown and bubbling.

BAKED SEA BREAM

WITH HERBS AND LEMON

SERVES 4

Two words followed us on our adventure: simple and natural. This dish does both well. Sea bream is easy to get here and in the Mediterranean and when it's good and banging fresh it's unbeatable. There will be some herb oil left over but it's a great thing to have in your kitchen.

2 large sea bream, scaled and gutted (about 400g each)
1 lemon, thinly sliced
salt and black pepper

Herb-infused oil
150ml olive oil
a few fresh sprigs of rosemary
a few sprigs of thyme
a few sprigs of sage
3 garlic cloves, sliced

First prepare the oil. Pour the olive oil into a small saucepan. Roughly chop half the rosemary, thyme and sage and add them to the saucepan, then add the sliced garlic. Heat the olive oil gently for a few minutes, watching to make sure the garlic doesn't take on anything but the lightest of colour. Leave the oil to cool down, then strain it into a jug or bottle. Reserve the garlic and herbs.

Preheat the oven to 200°C/Fan 180°C/Gas 6. Line a large roasting dish or tray with 2 sheets of foil, making sure you leave enough extra to fold the fish into a loose parcel. Drizzle some of the herb oil over the foil. Season the sea bream generously, inside and out, with salt and pepper, then stuff with the remaining herbs and half the lemon slices. Tuck half the remaining lemon slices under the fish and place the rest on top. Drizzle over a little more of the infused oil, then wrap the fish in the foil.

Bake the fish in the oven for about 20 minutes until it's cooked through and piping hot. Unwrap the fish and transfer them to a serving platter, drizzling over any juices that have collected in the foil. Drizzle over a little more of the infused oil and garnish with the reserved garlic and herbs. Serve immediately.

STUFFED MUSSELS

SERVES 4

We ate these for our first supper in Bonifacio in Corsica, so we just had to try cooking them ourselves. After a day with the fishermen collecting oysters and mussels, we took away a big bag of mussels and came up with this tasty dish. Large mussels work best but if you have a few tiny ones you can add the flesh to the larger shells. Some local recipes stuff them with minced chicken, but we like ours just like this.

1 bag of mussels (about 60)

150ml white wine or vermouth

1 large sprig of parsley

Stuffing

25g fine breadcrumbs

25g hard cheese that melts well – Corsican local cheese or mixture of Gruyère and Pecorino

2 tbsp finely chopped flatleaf parsley

1 tbsp finely chopped tarragon

1 tbsp finely chopped basil

3 garlic cloves, finely chopped

30ml olive oil

salt and black pepper

Wash the mussels well and scrape off any barnacles and beards. Discard any mussels that won't close completely when you give them a sharp tap. Put the wine or vermouth into a large lidded saucepan with the parsley and bring it to the boil. Add the mussels and cover the pan, then leave them to steam for 4–5 minutes or until they have opened fully. Discard any mussels that don't open. Preheat the oven to 200°C/Fan 180°C/Gas 6.

Remove each mussel from the pan and remove one of its shells. Sit the mussels on the half shell on a large baking tray. Drizzle over a little of the cooking liquor to keep them moist, then discard the rest of it.

Mix all the stuffing ingredients together and season to taste. Divide the stuffing between the mussels, placing it on top of the mussel flesh. Bake the mussels in the oven for 5 minutes until very lightly crisped up.

TROUT

WITH GARLIC BUTTER SAUCE

SERVES 4

With trout so cheap and plentiful it's well worth giving this one a go, and if like us you love garlic you'll find it's a little treasure. It's great with sautéed garlic potatoes or a nice risotto. Mmmmm – cook it tonight!

4 trout, filleted, skin on
1 tbsp flour
1 tsp herbes de Provence (or ½ tsp dried oregano, and pinches of dried sage and thyme)
up to 4 tbsp olive oil
4 garlic cloves, crushed
1 bay leaf
1 sprig of rosemary
1 sprig of thyme
250ml white wine
30g butter
2 tbsp flatleaf parsley, finely chopped
salt and black pepper

Check the trout for any little pin bones and pull them out with tweezers if necessary. Season the flour with salt and pepper and add the dried herbs. Mix thoroughly, then dust the trout fillets with the seasoned flour, patting off any excess.

Heat a tablespoon of the oil in a large frying pan. Add half the fillets, skin-side down, pressing the fish firmly as you add each fillet so it doesn't curl up. Cook them for 2–3 minutes until they are browned and come away from the pan easily, then turn them over and cook for another couple of minutes, flesh-side down. Remove the fillets from the pan and keep them warm while you cook the rest.

If the frying pan is quite dry, add a little more olive oil. Add the garlic and cook for a couple of minutes until it's softening but not taking on any colour. Turn up the heat then add the bay leaf, rosemary and thyme and pour in the wine. Season with salt and pepper. Let the wine bubble furiously until well reduced, then throw in the butter. Whisk until the butter has completely combined with the wine, then stir in the parsley. Serve the trout fillets with the sauce spooned over the top.

CHICKEN BREASTS

WITH CHERRIES

SERVES 4

We found loads of cherry recipes around the Med for both sweet and savoury dishes. This dish is very loosely based on a traditional Corsican recipe for songbirds – thrush or blackbirds – which are stuffed with cherries, wrapped in pancetta and then served with a cherry sauce. We didn't want to go stuffing blackbirds so we used chicken breasts instead!

1 tbsp olive oil
½ onion, finely chopped
½ tsp juniper berries
75g cherries, roughly chopped
200g sausage meat (we used 3 Toulouse sausages)
4 boneless chicken breasts, skinned
16 slices of pancetta
salt and black pepper

Cherry sauce
15g butter
½ onion, finely chopped
100ml red wine
200ml chicken stock
225g cherries, pitted and halved
1 tbsp cherry liqueur (optional)

Heat the oil in a frying pan, add the onion and sauté it until softened. Add the juniper berries and the cherries and continue to cook until most of the juice has disappeared. Remove the pan from the heat and leave to cool, then mix in the sausage meat. Preheat the oven to 200°C/Fan 180°C/Gas 6.

Take each chicken breast and place it smooth-side down. Remove the small fillet if it is still there. Cut down the centre of the breast, making sure you don't cut all the way through, then cut about 2.5cm into the flesh on either side of this cut to make a cavity.

Lay 4 slices of the pancetta on your work surface and put a chicken breast in the centre. Take a quarter of the sausage and stuff the cavity you have made. Place the fillet back on top. Pull the pancetta tightly round the chicken so the middle section is completely encased (there may be a little bit of chicken visible at the top and the bottom). Repeat to stuff the rest of the breasts in the same way. Put the stuffed breasts in a roasting tin and roast for 25–30 minutes until completely cooked through. Strain off any juices from the roasting tin.

Heat the butter in a frying pan, add the onion and sauté until softened. Set the roasting tin over the heat, pour in the wine and scrape up any sticky bits. Pour this, the reserved juices and the stock into the pan. Bring to the boil and simmer until reduced by half. Add the cherries and the liqueur, if using, and cook for 2–3 minutes until piping hot. Add any other liquid from the resting chicken. Slice the chicken breasts and serve with the sauce.

CHICKEN AND SAGE TRAYBAKE

SERVES 4

We always enjoy a traybake and this is a distinctly Mediterranean version, with all the herbs, olives, apricots and pumpkin. It makes a great family supper. We found that Corsicans eat a lot of pumpkin and there is lovely wild sage growing all over the island. This is good with some crusty bread or can we suggest a baked potato or two?

4 chicken legs or 8 thighs, skin on, bone in

2 red onions, cut into wedges

400g piece of pumpkin, peeled and cut into chunks

4 small, ripe apricots, quartered (optional)

1 garlic bulb, separated into cloves, unpeeled

bunch of fresh sage, roughly chopped

2 tbsp olive oil

50g green olives

salt and black pepper

Marinade

1 tbsp olive oil

juice and zest of 1 lemon

1 tsp dried sage

1 tsp dried oregano

3 garlic cloves, crushed

½ tsp chilli flakes

To serve

chopped sage, thyme and flatleaf parsley

lemon wedges

Put the chicken pieces in a bowl and season them with salt and pepper. Mix the ingredients for the marinade together and pour it over the chicken, rubbing it into and under the skin. Leave the chicken to marinate for at least an hour in the fridge, but preferably overnight.

Remove the chicken from the fridge half an hour before you want to cook it. Preheat the oven to 200°C/Fan 180°C/Gas 6.

Spread the onions, pumpkin, apricots, garlic and sage over the base of a roasting tin and season with salt and black pepper. Drizzle over the olive oil and mix thoroughly so everything is well coated. Put the chicken on top and drizzle over any remaining marinade.

Roast in the oven for 45–50 minutes until everything is tender and slightly charred round the edges and the chicken is cooked through. Add the olives for the last 5 minutes just to heat through. Serve sprinkled with plenty of herbs and with some lemon wedges on the side to squeeze over the chicken.

VEAL AND OLIVE STEW

SERVES 4–6

They have excellent veal in Corsica and this classic recipe is our homage to the veal farmer we met high in the hills on the island. We reckoned his was the best veal we'd ever tasted, but this recipe is also great made with British rose veal. The Corsicans often serve this stew over pasta but some new potatoes would be nice too.

1kg rose veal shoulder, cut into 4cm chunks

1 tbsp plain flour

3 tbsp olive oil

100g pancetta or streaky bacon lardons

2 onions, finely chopped

2 celery sticks, finely chopped

3 carrots, thinly sliced

4 garlic cloves, finely chopped

500ml white wine

100ml chicken stock

1 piece of pared lemon zest

2 bay leaves

1 large sprig of thyme

2 sprigs of rosemary

200g fresh tomatoes, peeled and finely chopped or puréed

50g green olives

salt and black pepper

Dust the veal pieces with flour and season them with salt and pepper. Heat a tablespoon of the olive oil in a large frying pan and sear the veal on both sides. Do this in a couple of batches, using another tablespoon of olive oil for the second batch. Set the veal aside.

Heat the remaining tablespoon of olive oil in a large flameproof casserole dish. Add the pancetta or bacon and fry it over a medium to high heat until crisp and brown. Some of the fat should also have rendered out. Add the onions, celery and carrots, then reduce the heat a little. Fry the vegetables gently for about 10 minutes, until they have taken on some colour and softened slightly.

Add the garlic and cook for a further couple of minutes, then add the veal to the casserole dish. Deglaze the frying pan with some of the wine and pour this over the veal, then add the rest of the wine to the casserole, along with the chicken stock. Add the lemon zest and herbs, then season with salt and pepper. Bring to the boil, then turn the heat down and put the lid on the dish. Simmer for about 45 minutes.

Add the tomatoes and olives and cook the stew for another half an hour, uncovered, to reduce the sauce a little. Serve with pasta, Corsican-style, or with new potatoes.

CORSICAN LAMB

SERVES 6

Give your Sunday roast the Mediterranean touch. Corsicans love their meat and cook it well and when you put this recipe with our British lamb you have something really special. The method is simple but the potatoes are to die for.

1.5kg lamb leg or shoulder, boned

1kg potatoes, thickly sliced into rounds

2 onions, sliced into crescents

2 garlic bulbs, split into cloves

a few sprigs of rosemary

4 bay leaves, lightly crumbled

1 tbsp juniper berries, lightly crushed

1 tbsp olive oil

250ml white wine

juice of 1 lemon

salt and black pepper

Preheat the oven to 220°C/Fan 200°C/Gas 7. Take the lamb out of the fridge a good hour before you want to start cooking it so it has time to come up to room temperature.

Layer the potatoes and onions over the base of a roasting tin. Season with salt and pepper and sprinkle in the garlic cloves, herbs and berries. Drizzle with a tablespoon of olive oil and mix everything thoroughly, before spreading it all out in an even layer. Pour over the white wine and lemon juice.

Season the lamb with salt and pepper and place it on top of the vegetables. Put it in the oven and immediately turn the heat down to 160°C/Fan 140°C/Gas 3. Roast for 2½–3 hours until the meat is very soft and tender.

Remove the lamb from the oven. Place it on a large, warmed serving platter, cover it with foil and leave it to rest for 20 minutes. Put the potatoes and onions back in the oven while the lamb rests so those that were covered by the lamb have a chance to crisp up a little.

Drizzle any juices from the resting lamb over the veg, then spoon them around the meat or into a separate dish. Serve immediately.

WILD BOAR CASSEROLE

SERVES 4-6

A rich meaty casserole with wild boar, mushrooms and chestnuts, this is food straight from the mountains of Corsica. Ideally, start this the day before so the marinade can work its magic, tenderising the meat and adding flavour. We know that wild boar isn't available at every corner shop but you can also make this with pork shoulder.

1kg wild boar

4 tbsp olive oil

100g pancetta or bacon, cut into lardons

1 large onion, sliced

2 celery sticks, sliced

3 garlic cloves, finely chopped

2 tbsp tomato purée

1 tbsp plain flour

150ml vermouth

25g dried porcini or wild mushrooms, soaked in a little warm water

300ml chicken stock

200g chestnuts (vacuum packed are fine)

chopped parsley, to serve

salt and black pepper

Marinade
500ml red wine

3 garlic cloves, crushed

1 tbsp juniper berries, lightly crushed

1 tsp black peppercorns

3 cloves, lightly crushed

2 sprigs of rosemary, roughly chopped

1 sprig of thyme, chopped

2 bay leaves, crumbled

Cut the wild boar meat into 4–5cm chunks and season them with salt. Mix all the marinade ingredients together in a large bowl, then add the meat. Make sure it is completely coated in the marinade, then cover and leave it to marinate in the fridge for several hours, preferably overnight.

Drain the wild boar, reserving the liquid. Brush off the marinade ingredients and reserve those too. Leave the boar to return to room temperature.

Heat half the oil in a large flameproof casserole dish. Sear the meat on all sides until well browned – you may need to do this in 2–3 batches, adding a little more oil in between. Remove each batch as it browns and set it aside.

Add the pancetta or bacon to the casserole dish and brown it briefly. Add the onion and celery and cook until they are starting to soften. Add the garlic and cook for another couple of minutes, then stir in the tomato purée and flour. Make sure everything is well combined, then pour over the vermouth. Continue to cook, stirring constantly, until the sauce has a consistency of a thin roux.

Add the marinade liquid and the rest of the marinade ingredients to the pan, along with the seared wild boar. Drain the porcini and rinse them, getting rid of any gritty bits. Finely chop the porcini and add them to the casserole dish. Pour in just enough stock to cover the meat, then season with salt and pepper. Bring to the boil, turn the heat down and cover. Simmer for 1–1½ hours until the meat is tender. Remove the lid and add the chestnuts. Simmer uncovered for another 20–30 minutes to reduce the sauce. Serve sprinkled with parsley.

SOUTH OF FRANCE

On to the South of France, that most glamorous stretch of Mediterranean coastline, and our first stop was Marseille, home to the some of the best fish dishes in the world such as bouillabaisse and bourride. We ate beautiful salads, fragrant fish soups and a tasty purée called brandade made from salt cod. We also loved the simple snacks such as panisse – fried chips made from chickpea flour, which went down so well with a glass of Provençal wine.

This is where we started to see the Moorish and Moroccan influences. And we were interested to see the growth in 'fusion' food – dishes that were essentially French and but with a North African touch. Inspired by this we came up with our spicy chicken and couscous fusion dish which you'll find on page 172.

One of our most fascinating experiences was in the Banyuls wine region where we went to see a lady who made the most amazing vinegar, and we tasted her fantastic product. Her business was tiny but highly acclaimed and she had an international reputation supplying a number of Michelin-starred restaurants as well as local customers. Her vinegar is so popular she can barely keep up with the demand. We noticed this respect for small producers all over the Mediterranean area and it is something people take great pride in.

SALADE NIÇOISE

SERVES 4

There are a million and one versions of this much-loved and typically Mediterranean salad. We've kept ours simple – no tuna or potatoes – and we love it. Put your sun hat on, pour a glass of chilled white wine to sip with this and you're in the South of France.

4 eggs
250g broad beans (podded) or 200g green beans
8 medium tomatoes, or 16–20 cherry tomatoes, at room temperature
½ large cucumber
½ red pepper
½ green pepper
½ red onion
small bunch of basil, leaves only
30g can of anchovies

Dressing
4 tbsp olive oil
1 tbsp red wine vinegar
1 garlic clove, crushed
salt and black pepper

Put the eggs in a small saucepan and cover them with water. Bring the water to the boil, then simmer the eggs for 6 minutes. Drain them and plunge them into iced water (or run them under a cold tap) until cool, then peel and set aside.

If using broad beans, blanch them for 2 minutes, then refresh them in cold water and peel away the grey skins. If using green beans, trim the tops, leaving the curly tails intact, then cook them for 3–4 minutes in boiling water until just tender. Refresh them in cold water.

Roughly chop the tomatoes, or halve them if using cherry tomatoes. Cut the cucumber in half lengthways, then slice it into half moons 4–5mm thick. Thinly slice the red and green peppers and the red onion. Put everything in a bowl and add the cooked beans and the basil leaves.

To make the dressing, drain the anchovies and put their oil with the olive oil in a small jug. Add the vinegar and garlic, then season with salt and pepper (you do still need the salt, despite the anchovies). Whisk well, then pour the dressing over the salad and mix thoroughly.

Serve the salad on a platter or in individual bowls. Quarter the eggs and add them, then thinly slice the anchovy fillets and drape them over the eggs and salad. Sprinkle with a little more black pepper and serve immediately.

WARM ENDIVE AND LENTIL SALAD

SERVES 4

This is the salad that's got more muscle than Vin Diesel! It's full of flavour and definitely a main event dish. You could also try sprinkling a few roasted hazelnuts over the top if you fancy.

4 heads of white or red endive/chicory
1 tbsp olive oil
100g salad leaves
100g cooked green lentils
100g cherry tomatoes, at room temperature, halved
75g soft French blue cheese (optional)
salt and black pepper

Dressing
2 tbsp walnut or olive oil
½ garlic clove, crushed
1 tbsp red wine vinegar
1 tsp Dijon mustard
1 tsp honey

First griddle the endive. Cut each endive in half, lengthways – the leaves should all still be attached to the base. Run the endives under cold water and shake off any excess. Toss them in the olive oil, then season with salt and pepper.

Heat a griddle until it's too hot to hold your hand over. Turn the heat down to medium, then grill the endive, cut-side down, until it's softened and lightly charred – this will take several minutes. Turn the endive halves over and continue to cook them on the other side. They should be charred and just tender when pierced with the point of a knife – you don't want them to break down.

Arrange the salad leaves on a serving platter or on 4 individual plates. Sprinkle over the lentils and cherry tomatoes, then add the griddled endive. Spoon or crumble over the cheese, if using.

Mix the dressing ingredients together, season well with salt and pepper and add a little water to thin it out if necessary. Drizzle the dressing over the salad, then serve immediately.

RATATOUILLE SALAD

SERVES 4

We're not great fans of stewed ratatouille, but this version, served as a warm salad, is epic and all the individual vegetables retain their shape and flavour. It's best if you can get quite skinny aubergines, but if you want a really quick meal you can make this with the grilled veggies available on the deli counter in supermarkets. The deep black wrinkly olives are best here – unpitted.

1 long, skinny aubergine, sliced into ½cm rounds

1 large courgette, cut on the diagonal into ½cm slices

olive oil, for brushing

1 floppy green or oak leaf lettuce or a mixture of salad leaves

1 roast red pepper (see p.320), peeled and pulled into strips

12 yellow cherry tomatoes, halved

12 black Provençal olives

salt and black pepper

Dressing

2 medium tomatoes, peeled

3 tbsp olive oil

1 garlic clove, finely chopped

sprig fresh oregano or marjoram, leaves only

small bunch of basil leaves, shredded

Sprinkle the aubergine and courgette slices with salt and leave them to stand in a colander for half an hour.

Pat the slices dry and brush them with olive oil. Heat a griddle until it's too hot to hold your hand over. Griddle the slices in batches until they are softened and have distinctive char lines. The courgettes will take 2–3 minutes on each side and the aubergines up to 4–5 minutes on each side. Let the veg cool to room temperature.

To make the warm tomato dressing, set a sieve over a bowl. Cut the tomatoes in half and pull out the cores and seeds. Press these through the sieve and try to extract as much juice as possible – a lot of the flavour is in the jelly around the seeds – then set it aside. Dice the tomato flesh.

Heat the olive oil in a small saucepan or frying pan and add the garlic. Let it cook gently for 2–3 minutes without taking on any colour, then turn up the heat and add the diced tomatoes and the reserved juice. Turn the tomatoes over in the olive oil for no more than 30 seconds – the tomatoes should stay quite distinct from the olive oil, not make a homogenous sauce. Remove the pan from the heat, season the dressing with salt and pepper and stir in the herbs.

To assemble the salad, arrange the lettuce or salad leaves on a large serving platter. Add the aubergines, courgettes, red pepper and cherry tomatoes and toss very lightly. Sprinkle the olives on top and drizzle over the warm dressing, then serve at once.

TAPENADE

MAKES ONE POT

We went head to head in a taste test near Nîmes with this olive dip. One of us did the classic with black olives and the other made a version with green, but we both agreed that the classic won hands down. The dry slightly wrinkled black olives are best here – don't use the pitted or pickled ones.

200g black olives
50g capers
2 anchovy fillets, finely chopped
1 garlic clove, crushed
juice of ½ lemon
1 tsp red wine vinegar
pinch of chilli flakes or cayenne
75ml olive oil
1 tbsp finely chopped flatleaf parsley
1 tsp finely chopped thyme leaves
black pepper

Remove the stones from the olives using an olive or cherry pitter, or just cut round the stone with a very sharp knife – be very careful, of course. If using the wrinkly sort of olive, the stone will usually pop out easily if you tear the olive open. Others may require more effort.

If the capers you have are packed in salt, pour over just-boiled water to dissolve the salt, then rinse them thoroughly.

Put the olives, capers, anchovy fillets, garlic, lemon juice and red wine vinegar in a food processor. Season with pepper and add the chilli flakes or cayenne – it is unlikely you will need salt. Pulse the mixture, scraping it down the sides of the bowl regularly until everything has combined into a coarse purée.

For a smooth tapenade, leave the motor running and gradually drizzle in the olive oil. For a coarser paste, add all the olive oil at once and blitz very briefly just to combine. Taste the mixture and adjust the seasoning as you like, then stir in the herbs. Scoop the tapenade into a jar and store it in the fridge. Serve on toast, with sticks of raw veg – whatever you like.

BRANDADE DE MORUE

SALT COD PURÉE

MAKES A BIG BOWLFUL

This is one of the best ways of using salt cod. We cooked this while filming our Med series and it's one of those classic South of France dishes – light, fluffy, creamy, rich and tasty, and wonderful piled on to a bit of toasted baguette. It makes a great beer snack on a sunny day whether you're in Nîmes or Newcastle. We used salt cod on the bone, but if you buy a filleted piece you need about 300g.

500g salt cod
500ml milk
2 bay leaves
2 garlic cloves,
thinly sliced
a few peppercorns
½ tsp fennel seeds
1 piece of thinly pared
lemon zest
400g potatoes, peeled
and cut into chunks
100ml single cream
75ml olive oil

To serve
thin slices of French
bread, toasted
grating of nutmeg
1–2 tbsp olive oil
a few slices of truffle
(optional)

First soak the cod – you will need to start this a full day ahead. Put the cod in a large container and cover it with cold water. Leave it to soak at room temperature for 24 hours, changing the water at least 4 times.

Drain the cod and put it in a saucepan. Cover with fresh water and bring it to the boil, then simmer for 5 minutes and drain. Repeat this process. Put the cod back in the saucepan but this time cover it with the milk. Add the bay leaves, garlic, peppercorns, fennel seeds and zest. Heat gently until the milk is almost boiling, then turn the heat down and leave the cod to simmer for 10 minutes. Remove the pan from the heat and leave the fish to cool in the milk.

Put the potatoes in a pan and cover them with water. Bring them to the boil and simmer for about 10 minutes until tender, then drain. Strain the cod, reserving 50ml of the milk, but discarding the bay and other aromatics. Remove any skin and bone from the cod, then crush the flakes lightly with a fork.

Put the fish and potatoes in a food processor with the reserved milk and the cream. Blend until the mixture is becoming smooth, then gradually drizzle in the oil while the motor is running until you have a smooth, well-emulsified mixture. Alternatively, you can mash the cod with a fork, or pound it using a pestle and mortar, then gradually incorporate the reserved milk. Mash the potatoes with the cream, mix everything together, then slowly work in the olive oil. Serve on toasted bread with a little nutmeg, a drizzle of oil and even a few slices of truffle, if you fancy.

FOUGASSE

PROVENÇAL BREAD

MAKES 6 SMALL BREADS

This bread is the French version of the Italian focaccia (see page 64). With its distinctive shape which gives just the right amount of crunch, it's the true tear-and-share sunshine bread and you need a pile of these on every Mediterranean table. It's good with a nice oil and vinegar dip.

500g strong white bread flour, plus extra for dusting

5g instant yeast

1 tsp sea salt

2 tbsp olive oil, plus extra for greasing

350ml warm water

You can make this in a stand mixer or by hand. If making it in a stand mixer, put the flour and yeast in the bowl with the salt, then drizzle in the oil. With the motor running, gradually incorporate the water. The dough will seem very wet to start with, but keep kneading with the dough hook for about 10 minutes and it will become very elastic, although still very soft.

If making the dough by hand, combine the flour, yeast and salt in a bowl, then add all the oil and water until you have a sticky dough. Turn it out on to a floured work surface and knead the dough by stretching it away from you and folding it back until it is soft and elastic. Put the dough in a lightly oiled bowl and cover it with a damp tea towel. Leave it for at least an hour until it has doubled in size.

Preheat your oven to its highest setting and put a couple of up-turned baking trays into the oven to heat up. Turn the dough out on to a floured work surface and then knock it back.

Cut the dough in half, then cut each half into 3 pieces. Pat each piece of dough into a rough rectangle – it will spring back to start with but keep going. Take a pastry scraper (or a sharp knife) and cut down the centre. Stretch out the hole. Cut several more holes diagonally on either side, each time stretching the hole with your fingers. Having floury fingers helps.

Dust the baking trays with flour. Carefully place the pieces of dough on the trays, then put them in the oven and bake the bread for 10–12 minutes until golden brown. If you have a water spray bottle, spritz the inside of the oven when you put the dough in – this will help develop the crust. Remove and serve warm or cool.

LEEKS NIÇOISE

SERVES 4 AS A SIDE OR STARTER

This is best made with baby leeks but you could also use some fat spring onions instead. It's a wonderful Provençal celebration of the leek – worthy of Tom Jones himself.

16–20 baby leeks, trimmed

2 tbsp olive oil

2 garlic cloves, crushed

150ml white wine

a few sprigs of thyme, leaves only

a few sprigs of oregano, leaves only

2 bay leaves

2 medium tomatoes (about 200g), peeled and chopped

pinch of sugar (optional)

50g Niçoise olives, whole or pitted

zest of ½ lemon

a few parsley leaves, finely chopped (optional)

salt and black pepper

Trim the leeks, discarding any very coarse leaves, then cut each one lengthways from the top down the centre for 2–3cm. Run the cut leeks under the tap, splaying out the tops to make sure they are thoroughly clean.

Heat the olive oil in a frying pan that has a lid. Add the leeks and cook them over a high heat for 3–4 minutes until they are very lightly browned on all sides. Keep shaking the pan regularly. Turn down the heat to medium, then add the garlic. Cook gently for another couple of minutes, then pour the wine into the pan. Season with salt and pepper.

Bring the wine to the boil and simmer for a few minutes until the leeks are just tender, then add the herbs and tomatoes. Cover the pan and turn the heat down to low. Continue to cook for 10 minutes to let the tomatoes break down, then remove the lid. Taste and adjust the seasoning – if your tomatoes are not very ripe you may want to add a pinch of sugar. Add the olives and lemon zest and cook for another 5 minutes until the sauce is reduced.

Allow the leeks to cool to room temperature, then sprinkle with parsley, if using, and serve with plenty of bread to mop up the juices.

PANISSE

CHICKPEA FLOUR CHIPS

SERVES 4

These little beauties are the Mediterranean version of chips and they are brilliant. They should be eaten straight out of the pan and the aim is for them to seem as light as air – almost as if they are all crust, no centre; the best beer snack ever. Gram or chickpea flour is cheap and available in supermarkets.

olive oil
200g chickpea (gram) flour
½ tsp salt
750ml tepid water
salt

Lightly oil a 30 x 20cm roasting tin. Sift the flour into a saucepan and add the salt. Whisk in the tepid water – trickle it in very gradually to start with until you have a thick, smooth paste and all the flour is worked in, then pour the rest of the water in more quickly. When all the water has been added to the flour and you have a runny, lump-free batter, put the saucepan over a medium heat. Cook, stirring constantly – this is important as the flour can easily catch on the base of the saucepan if left unattended and lumps can form. Nothing much will happen for a few minutes, but then the batter will quickly start to thicken and will continue to do so until you have a thick paste, the texture of thick custard.

Remove the pan from the heat and immediately spread the mixture over the oiled tin, making sure it is as even as possible. Cover it with a tea towel or cling film and leave it to set for about half an hour or until firm to the touch.

When you are ready to cook the panisse, cut the mixture into fat chips. Pour olive oil to a depth of about 1cm into a large frying pan. Heat the oil over a medium to high heat, then add a batch of the chips – you'll probably need to cook them in 3 or 4 batches so you don't overcrowd the pan. Fry the chips for 3–4 minutes on each side, flipping them over half way through, then drain them on kitchen paper. When cooked, they should be a deep golden brown and slightly cracked in places. Sprinkle with salt and eat immediately – these do not keep well, but they don't often get the chance!

SOCCA

CHICKPEA FLOUR PANCAKES

MAKES 2 LARGE SOCCA

We did feature these great chickpea flour pancakes in our last diet book – 'Go Veggie' – but we couldn't resist including a full-fat version here. We've tried a slightly different method of cooking them too to get that authentic charred smoky taste.

150g chickpea (gram) flour
1 tsp herbes de Provence, plus extra for serving
2 tbsp olive oil
sea salt and black pepper

Sift the flour into a bowl. Add plenty of salt and pepper and the herbs. Mix thoroughly, then gradually whisk in 250ml of water until you have a smooth batter with the consistency of double cream.

Stir in a tablespoon of the olive oil and whisk vigorously until it is all mixed in. Leave the batter to rest for at least half an hour before frying.

To make 2 large socca, preheat your grill to its highest setting. Heat a large, preferably ovenproof frying pan until it's very hot – you can do this under the grill if the pan is ovenproof, otherwise set it over a high heat on the hob. Drizzle over a few drops of oil and brush it over the whole surface of the frying pan. Pour in half the batter and swirl it to make sure it covers the whole base of the pan. Leave the batter to set, then instead of flipping the pancake, put the pan under the grill for a few minutes. The aim is to get a crisp, very slightly charred pancake.

Remove the pancake and keep it warm, then repeat with the remaining batter. To serve, sprinkle with sea salt and a few more herbes de Provence. You can cut the socca into wedges or leave them whole so people can tear off pieces at the table.

QUICHE PROVENÇALE

SERVES 6-8

When it comes to quiche we've always been quite traditional up until now. But when you get to the Med you tend to loosen up and take in a few local influences so this one is a bit different. We think it really works.

1 large courgette, thinly sliced into rounds

3 tbsp olive oil

1 tsp herbes de Provence

150g cherry tomatoes, halved

½ onion, very finely chopped

5 eggs

150ml double cream

150ml whole milk

a few oregano leaves

2 sprigs of tarragon, finely chopped

a few basil leaves, roughly torn

salt and black pepper

Pastry

225g plain flour, plus extra for dusting

pinch of salt

65g butter, chilled

60g lard, chilled

2–3 tbsp iced water

First make the pastry. Put the flour into a bowl and add a pinch of salt. Rub in the butter and lard with your fingertips until the mixture resembles fine breadcrumbs. Drizzle in the water a little at a time, just using as much as you need to form a dough – the less water, the shorter the pastry. Cut the water in with a knife, then use your hands to lightly knead the dough into a smooth ball. Wrap it in cling film and chill it in the fridge for at least an hour.

Preheat the oven to 180°C/Fan 160°C/Gas 4. Lightly flour a work surface and roll out the pastry into a round large enough to line a 25cm flan dish. Trim off any large pieces of overhanging pastry. Prick the pastry base with a fork, then cover it with baking paper and fill it with baking beans. Bake the pastry case in the preheated oven for 15 minutes, then remove the beans and paper and bake for another 5 minutes. Remove it from the oven and leave to cool down.

To make the filling, put the courgette slices on a baking tray and drizzle them with oil. Sprinkle them with salt and herbes de Provence. Roast the courgette slices for 10 minutes, then add the tomatoes. Roast for another 10 minutes, by which time the courgette should be lightly browned in patches and the tomatoes will have wrinkled a little and lost some moisture. Remove the tray from the oven and leave to cool.

Put the cooked pastry case in its dish on a baking tray. Sprinkle the onion over the base of the pastry case, then top with the courgette and tomatoes. Beat the eggs in a bowl, then add the cream and milk. Make sure everything is well combined without letting it froth. Season with salt and pepper. Pour the eggs, cream and milk mixture into the pastry case, then sprinkle with the herbs. Turn the oven down to 170°C/Fan 150°C/Gas 3½ and bake the quiche for 25–30 minutes until lightly browned. It should still be slightly wobbly in the middle when you take it out. Serve it warm or at room temperature, with a green salad on the side.

PISSALADIÈRE

SERVES 6–8

This was Si's holiday favourite as a child. It's one of those classic dishes that just works, with the anchovies, olives, onions and thyme all working their magic. We find that making the dough with plain flour, not strong bread flour, makes a big difference. It means that the pissaladière is good to eat cold as well as hot, as the dough doesn't go too hard. You do have to cook the onions for a long time to get them to the right texture but it's worth it, we promise.

Dough

250g plain flour
1 tsp salt
5g instant dried yeast
1 tbsp honey
50ml olive oil
125ml warm water

Topping

2 tbsp olive oil
knob of butter
1.25g onions, thinly sliced
a few thyme leaves (optional)
2 x 100g jars of anchovies, drained
150g black olives, pitted
salt

To make the dough, put the flour in a bowl and add the salt. Whisk, then add the yeast. Mix the honey with the oil and water, then pour this over the flour. Mix until you have a sticky dough, then turn it out and knead until soft. Stretch out a small piece of dough until you can see through it – if you are able to do this it shows that the gluten is developed enough and the dough is ready. Put it back in the bowl and cover it with a damp tea towel, then leave it for at least an hour to double in size.

Meanwhile, make the topping. Heat the olive oil and butter in a very large frying pan. When the butter has melted and is foaming, add the onions and thyme, if using. Season with salt and stir carefully until the onions reduce in volume. They will collapse quite quickly.

Continue to cook over a low to medium heat for 45 minutes to an hour, stirring regularly. The onions will start to caramelise on the base of the pan so scrape them up regularly as you stir. You will end up with a pan of very soft, almost puréed, golden-brown onions. If you prefer, you can cover the pan and let the onions sweat for a similar time. They will collapse in the same way but will be lighter in colour. Preheat the oven to 230°C/Fan 210°C/Gas 8.

Knock the dough back and shape it to fill a large baking tray – it should be about 35 x 25cm. Spread the onions over the dough, leaving a narrow border. Add the anchovies in a lattice pattern – or more free form if you prefer. Add the olives at intervals, then drizzle with a little more olive oil if you like. Bake in the preheated oven for 20–25 minutes until the dough is cooked through. Cool slightly, then cut into slices and serve.

BOUILLABAISSE

SERVES 4-6

Pack your bags – you're off to the South of France with this recipe. It's so good you can imagine yourself at a restaurant in Marseille. Fennel, pastis, saffron and the rouille sauce all work brilliantly together to make a classy classic that's more than worth the effort.

Broth

12 large whole prawns
1 tbsp olive oil
1 tbsp tomato purée
250ml white wine
4 medium tomatoes, roughly chopped
2 pieces of pared orange zest
pinch of saffron
sprigs of flatleaf parsley, thyme, tarragon and fresh oregano
1.5 litres fish stock (see p. 316)

Soup

2 tbsp olive oil
1 fennel bulb
2 leeks, sliced into rounds
500g mixture of white fish, such as monkfish, red mullet, cut into chunks
24 mussels, washed
1–2 tsp pastis (optional)
a few flat leaf parsley and tarragon leaves, finely chopped

First make the broth for the soup. Remove the heads and shells from the prawns and set them aside. Pull out the digestive tract – the dark line – from the prawns. Heat the oil in a large saucepan and sear the prawns very quickly on both sides. Remove them and set them aside. Let them cool, then pop them in the fridge until needed. Add the prawn heads and shells to the saucepan. Cook over a high heat until they have turned pink, then stir in the tomato purée and continue to cook for another couple of minutes.

Pour over the wine and allow it to bubble fiercely. When it has reduced by half, add the tomatoes, zest, saffron and herbs. Pour over the fish stock. Bring to the boil, then turn down the heat and simmer for 15 minutes. Remove the pan from the heat and strain the stock, pushing through as much of the tomato as you can to give the broth a little texture.

Meanwhile, heat the olive oil in a large flameproof casserole dish. Trim the fennel and cut it in half lengthways, then into thin strips – hopefully the strips will be held together at the base. Add the fennel and leeks to the dish. Add a splash of water and cover. Cook over a medium heat, stirring every so often, until the fennel and leeks have softened and started to take on some colour around the edges.

Pour over the strained broth and simmer for 10 minutes until the vegetables are completely tender. Drop in the fish, the reserved prawns and the mussels, then cover and leave for 3–4 minutes. The fish should be just cooked through and the mussels should have opened – discard any that don't. Stir in the pastis, if using.

Rouille

1 small slice of bread or 50g breadcrumbs
50ml broth (see method)
2 garlic cloves
½ tsp cayenne or hot chilli powder
1 tbsp tomato purée
2 egg yolks
250ml olive oil
salt and black pepper

Croutons

12 thin slices of baguette
1 garlic clove, cut in half
100g Gruyère cheese, grated

Make the rouille while the broth is cooking. Put the bread or breadcrumbs into a bowl. Skim off about 50ml of the broth, catching as much of the deep orange oil as you can – this will help with the colour of the rouille – and add it to the bread. Soak the bread for 10 minutes, then squeeze out any excess. Put the bread in a food processor with the garlic, cayenne or chilli, tomato purée and egg yolks. Season with salt and pepper. Blitz until smooth, then with the motor still running, gradually add the olive oil. Do this one drop at a time to start with until the mixture comes together, then add it in a slow but steady stream. You should end up with a creamy orange sauce with the texture of mayonnaise.

To make the croutons, preheat your grill to its highest setting. Lightly toast the slices of bread in a toaster then rub each one with the cut side of the garlic. Add the cheese and put the toasts under the grill for 2–3 minutes until the cheese has melted. Serve the fish, ladled into bowls and sprinkled with herbs, with the rouille and croutons on the side.

FISH WITH SAUCE VIERGE

SERVES 4

You can use any fish for this, but it works best with something white-fleshed and non-oily as the sauce is so oil rich. Sea bream or sea bass are both great but any white fish fillet or steak would work. Sauce vierge is a delicious herby sauce that is brilliant with fish.

4 fish fillets or steaks (about 150g each)

olive oil, for frying

salt and black pepper

Sauce vierge

100ml olive oil

1 shallot, very finely chopped

1 garlic clove, finely chopped

½ tsp coriander seeds, lightly crushed

4 medium tomatoes, peeled and finely diced

juice of ½ lemon

small bunch of flatleaf parsley, finely chopped

small bunch of basil leaves, finely shredded

1 tbsp capers

To make the sauce vierge, put the olive oil in a saucepan and heat it gently. Add the shallot and sauté until very soft and translucent – it should almost disintegrate into the oil. Add the garlic and coriander seeds and cook for another minute, then add the tomatoes and lemon juice. Continue to cook very gently for about 10 minutes to allow the tomatoes to break down a little and the flavours to blend. Keep it warm.

Season the fish on both sides with salt and pepper. Add a drizzle of olive oil to a large frying pan and heat until it's too hot to hold your hand over comfortably. Add the fillets, skin-side down and cook until you see the flesh is turning opaque up the sides and the skin is browning around the edges. Flip the fish over and cook for another minute.

Stir the parsley, basil and capers into the sauce. Serve the fish with the sauce spooned over the top.

BOURRIDE

FISH STEW WITH AIOLI

SERVES 4–6

This is our version of bourride, a kind of fish chowder that was cooked for us in Marseille. The lady who made it used monkfish but any firm white fish, such as sea bream or red mullet, will do. You'll notice there's only one clove of garlic in the aioli – when garlic is raw a little goes a long way.

2 tbsp olive oil
1 onion, finely chopped
3 garlic cloves, crushed
1 tbsp fennel seeds
2 bay leaves
3 sprigs of flatleaf parsley
250ml white wine
2 tomatoes, roughly chopped
1.5 litres fish stock (see p.316)
500g new or salad potatoes, thickly sliced
2 leeks, white part only, finely sliced
750g skinned white fish fillets, cut into chunks
salt and black or white pepper

Aioli

1 garlic clove, crushed
3 egg yolks
1 tbsp white wine vinegar
250ml mild olive oil or sunflower oil
squeeze of lemon juice

To serve

4–8 thick slices of French baguette, toasted
2 tbsp chopped parsley

First make the aioli. Put the garlic in a food processor with the egg yolks and the vinegar. Add salt and finely ground black or white pepper. With the motor running, start drizzling in the oil, a few drops at a time, until the mixture starts to emulsify. Then, start adding the oil in a slow, steady stream until you have used it all and the sauce has the texture of mayonnaise. Taste for seasoning and add lemon juice if the sauce needs it.

Next make the broth. Heat the olive oil in a large saucepan and add the onion. Sauté for about 10 minutes until it's soft and translucent, then add the garlic, fennel seeds and herbs. Turn up the heat and add the white wine. Bring it to the boil and reduce by two thirds, then add the tomatoes and stock. Simmer for 15 minutes, uncovered, then strain the broth through a coarse sieve, pushing through as much of the vegetables as possible.

Return the broth to the pan and season it with salt and pepper. Bring it to the boil and add the potatoes and leeks. Cover the pan and simmer for 15 minutes until the vegetables are just tender, then add the fish. Simmer for another 3–4 minutes, then remove the pan from the heat.

Put a couple of pieces of toasted baguette in each bowl. Very carefully remove the fish and vegetables from the broth and put them on the toast.

Take half the aioli and put it into a bowl. Add a ladleful of the broth to it and whisk until smooth, then pour the mixture back into the pan. Put the pan back over the heat and warm the soup through for a few minutes until it has thickened very slightly and has a silky texture. Don't let it come to the boil. Taste for seasoning, then ladle some broth into each bowl. Sprinkle with finely chopped parsley and serve the aioli on the side for everyone to spoon over their bowlful.

MEDITERRANEAN SEAFOOD SALAD

SERVES 4

This simple salad has a wonderful aniseedy flavour from the pastis, but you can leave it out if you aren't keen. This is a great recipe that you can make your own – toss in some steamed clams if you fancy or maybe a few mussels. It's the cooking juices added to the salad dressing that really work the magic.

1 small red onion, very thinly sliced

20 large prawns, peeled

250g squid, cleaned

2 tbsp olive oil

2 garlic cloves, crushed

½ tsp cayenne

½ fennel bulb, very thinly sliced, widthways

¼ cucumber, very thinly sliced on the diagonal

6 radishes, finely sliced into rounds

12 cherry tomatoes, halved

50g rocket leaves

50g frisee lettuce or similar

a few small basil leaves

a few small mint leaves

salt and black pepper

Dressing

2 tbsp olive oil

1 tsp pastis or similar (optional)

juice of ½ lemon

¼ tsp cayenne

First put the slices of onion in a bowl of iced water and leave them to soak for half an hour. This removes any bitterness.

To butterfly the prawns, cut along the back of each one, removing the digestive tract as you do so, then flatten the prawn out. Don't worry if you cut right through at the narrowest tip of the tail. Make sure the squid is thoroughly clean by running it under the tap and pulling away any fine membrane, then pat it dry. Cut the body of the squid into rings. If the tentacles are large, cut them in half lengthways but otherwise leave them whole.

Heat the olive oil in a large frying pan and add the garlic. Cook it, while stirring constantly, until it has softened and looks translucent but hasn't taken on any colour. Toss the prawns and squid in the cayenne and season them well with salt and pepper. Add them to the hot pan and cook them very quickly, turning them over after a minute, until the squid is opaque and the prawns have turned pink. Remove them from the pan and set aside. Deglaze the frying pan with a splash of water and tip the pan juices into a bowl.

Drain the onion. Put it in a large salad bowl with the fennel, cucumber, radishes, tomatoes and salad leaves. Toss thoroughly and season with salt and pepper.

Make the dressing by mixing the olive oil into the bowl of pan juices, then add the pastis, if using, the lemon juice and cayenne. Stir the prawns and squid into the dressing and add them to the salad. Toss again to combine and garnish with a few basil and mint leaves. Serve immediately.

PROVENÇAL FISH SOUP

SERVES 4–6

Unlike bourride and bouillabaisse, which both contain pieces of fish and shellfish, this soup is velvety smooth and rich. It really is worth making your own fish stock (page 316) for this one and your kitchen will smell like the best in Marseille.

2 tbsp olive oil

1 leek

1 onion, finely chopped

½ fennel bulb, finely sliced

1 celery stick, finely sliced

1 roasted red pepper (see p.322), cut into strips

1 red chilli, finely diced or ½ tsp hot chilli powder

4 garlic cloves, finely chopped

250ml white wine

pinch of saffron, soaked in a little warm water

1 tsp fennel seeds

1 bouquet garni (see method)

150g whole North Atlantic prawns

500g tomatoes, chopped or 400g can of tomatoes

1 litre fish stock (see p.316)

200g white fish fillets

1 tbsp pastis (optional)

salt and black pepper

To serve

rouille (see p.159)

croutons (see p.159)

Heat the olive oil in a large saucepan. Trim the leek and take off the outer layer – you will need this for the bouquet garni. Finely slice the rest of the leek and add it to the pan with the onion, fennel and celery. Cook the vegetables over a medium heat, stirring regularly, until they start to take on some colour and caramelise around the edges. Add the red pepper, chilli or chilli powder and the garlic and continue to cook for a few more minutes.

Turn up the heat and pour over the wine. Let it bubble until it has reduced by half and add the saffron and fennel seeds. Then add the bouquet garni (see below) to the pan with the prawns and tomatoes. Cook for 10 minutes until the tomatoes have given off most of their liquid and reduced down, then pour the stock into the pan and season with salt and pepper.

Bring the soup to the boil, then turn the heat down and simmer for half an hour, adding the white fish for the last 5 minutes or so. Take the pan off the heat and leave the soup to cool down a little. Remove the bouquet garni, then blitz the soup in a blender – or with a stick blender – until smooth. Push it through a sieve back into the saucepan and check for seasoning. Add the pastis, if using, then reheat the soup until piping hot. Serve with rouille and croutons.

Bouquet garni

Take 1 piece of pared orange zest, 2 bay leaves, 1 parsley sprig and 1 thyme sprig. Wrap them together with a leek leaf and tie securely.

PROVENÇAL BEEF DAUBE

SERVES 6

We were inspired to cook this great beef and red wine stew, Provence style, by seeing the black bulls of the Camargue. Any leftovers make really good beef ragù – just shred the beef, cook it down with some tomatoes and serve over some pasta.

1.5kg beef brisket, trimmed of excess fat
4 tbsp olive oil
150g bacon lardons
1 onion, finely chopped
2 tbsp tomato purée
up to 600ml beef stock
150g black olives
salt and black pepper

Marinade
2 onions, finely sliced
4 carrots, cut into 1cm rounds
2 celery sticks, cut into 1cm slices
6 garlic cloves, finely chopped
1 bottle of red wine
100ml brandy or cognac
50ml red wine vinegar

Bouquet garni
2 bay leaves
2 large sprigs of thyme
a few sprigs of parsley
strip of pared orange zest
2 cloves
1 tsp black peppercorns
4cm cinnamon stick

Cut the beef into large 6cm chunks and put them in a large bowl. Sprinkle it with salt, then add the marinade ingredients. Tie the ingredients for the bouquet garni in a piece of muslin and add it to the bowl, then cover the bowl and put it in the fridge. Leave the beef to marinate for at least 6 hours, but preferably overnight.

Drain the meat, reserving the liquid and the rest of the marinade ingredients. Pat the meat dry and brush off any garlic. Heat half the olive oil in a large frying pan and sear the meat in batches until it's all well browned. Deglaze the base of the frying pan with a little of the marinade liquid and set it aside.

Add the remaining oil to a large flameproof casserole dish. Add the bacon lardons and fry them over a high heat for a few minutes until crisp and brown. Add the onion, turn the heat down to medium and cook it for about 10 minutes until softened and lightly coloured. Stir in the tomato purée, then add the beef to the dish and stir.

Strain the marinade and pour the liquid into the dish along with the deglazing juices from the frying pan. Bring everything to the boil and simmer until the liquid has reduced by about a third, then add the vegetables from the marinade. Add enough of the beef stock to just cover the beef. Bring back to the boil, then turn the heat down low, cover the dish with a lid and simmer for about 3 hours.

If you can, leave this overnight once it's cooked, as when everything is cold it is much easier to skim off the fat. Otherwise, skim off some of the fat, which will collect at the top, as best you can. Add the olives, then simmer, uncovered, for a further hour to reduce the sauce. If you want to thicken the sauce more, mix a tablespoon each of softened butter and flour and whisk it in little by little towards the end of cooking time. This is great served with rice.

ROAST LAMB

WITH LAVENDER AND MEDITERRANEAN HERBS

SERVES 6-8

A main event roast, this has a distinctive – and delicious – aroma of lavender, which takes you straight to Provence and that amazing dry, herby, sunny smell in the air. Lavender works really well with lamb and when combined with the other herbs it makes the most fragrant roast you've ever tasted. Take care adding the lavender, though, and if the variety you have seems strong, add a little less to the paste.

1 leg of lamb (about 2.5kg), bone in
2 onions, sliced into rounds
a few lavender heads
100ml white wine

Paste
4 garlic cloves, peeled
4 heads of fresh lavender, purple petals only
4 sprigs of fresh rosemary, leaves only
4 sprigs of fresh thyme, leaves only
1 tsp dried oregano
1 tsp dried sage
1 tbsp olive oil
salt and black pepper

Remove the lamb from the fridge at least an hour before you want to start roasting it so it can come up to room temperature. Weigh the lamb and work out how long you will need to cook it for. For rare meat you will need to cook it for 10 minutes per 500g; for medium rare, 12 minutes; for medium, 15 minutes; and for well done, 18 minutes.

Preheat the oven to its highest setting while you make the paste for the lamb. Put everything in a food processor and blitz it to a rough, green and purple-flecked paste. Season with salt and pepper. Cut deep slits all over the lamb, then push the paste into the slits – use a small teaspoon if that helps. Rub any excess over the surface of the lamb.

Arrange the onions and lavender heads over the base of a roasting tin and place the lamb on top. Add the wine and another 100ml of water. Roast the lamb in the preheated oven for 20 minutes, then turn the temperature down to 180°C/Fan 160°C/Gas 4 and continue to roast for the time you have worked out.

Remove the lamb from the oven, place it on a platter and cover it loosely with foil. Leave it to rest for at least 20 minutes. Strain off the fat from the roasting tin – you will find if you leave it to cool for a few minutes, it will set and be much easier to skim off. Set the onions aside. Pour the remaining pan juices into a small saucepan and reheat them. Serve the juices with the lamb and onions.

MEDITERRANEAN ROAST CHICKEN

SERVES 4-6

The chicken needs its trip to the sun too and this is the perfect dish to serve to your chums when you are fed up with stuffing and roasties. Tuck into this, served with some salad and a heap of crusty bread to dip into the juices.

1 chicken (about 1.5kg)
a few sprigs of fresh thyme
a few sprigs each of oregano, lemon thyme, flatleaf parsley and tarragon
3 lemons
500g baby new potatoes
4 shallots, peeled
1 bulb of garlic, broken into cloves, unpeeled
2 tbsp olive oil
250ml white wine
75g green olives, unpitted
salt and black pepper

Salad
2 heads of floppy green lettuce

Dressing
2 tbsp olive oil
1 tbsp red wine vinegar
1 tsp mustard

Preheat the oven to 220°C/Fan 200°C/Gas 7. Take the chicken out of the fridge and leave it to come up to room temperature before you start roasting it. Season the inside of the chicken with salt and pepper. Take half the herbs and stuff them into the cavity of the chicken. Cut one of the lemons in half and stuff this into the chicken too.

Bring a pan of water to the boil and blanch the potatoes for about 3 minutes, then drain. Cut any that are on the large side in half. Cut the shallots in half and put them in the base of the roasting tin. Add the garlic cloves and the blanched potatoes. Zest and juice one of the remaining lemons and mix with the olive oil. Strip all the leaves from the remaining herbs and chop them finely, then mix with the olive oil and lemon and season with salt and pepper. Rub a generous amount of this over the chicken and drizzle the rest over the vegetables. Slice the third lemon and add it to the vegetables.

Pour the wine over the vegetables and place the chicken on top. Roast it in the hot oven for 20 minutes, then turn the oven down to 180°C/Fan 160°C/Gas 4 and roast for another hour. Turn the potatoes over halfway through the cooking time and add the olives. Check the chicken is cooked by piercing the thickest part of the leg with a skewer – the juices should run clear – or use a probe thermometer; the temperature should read 75°C. The outer layers of the shallots will have caramelised and the potatoes will be just tender.

Remove the chicken and vegetables from the pan. Cover the chicken with foil and leave it to rest for 20 minutes. Drain off the contents of the roasting tin and reheat them in a saucepan. Tear up the lettuce and put it in a salad bowl. Mix the dressing ingredients together and season with salt and pepper, then toss with the salad leaves. Serve the chicken with the vegetables, olives and lemon slices with the pan juices and the dressed salad on the side.

SPICED CHICKEN

WITH COUSCOUS

SERVES 4

We love a classic chicken Provençal but for this one we have taken our inspiration from the Moors. It's like an exotic bazaar full of herbs and spices and it's a dish you simply can't stop eating.

2–3 tbsp olive oil

4 chicken legs, or 8 thighs, skin on and bone in

1 red onion, sliced into wedges

1 red pepper, deseeded and thickly sliced

3 garlic cloves, finely chopped

1 tsp ground cumin

1 tsp ground coriander

1 tsp ground cinnamon

½ tsp ground cardamom

½ tsp ground turmeric

½ tsp chilli powder (optional)

a few sprigs of oregano, leaves only

zest of 1 lemon

250ml chicken stock

4 medium tomatoes, peeled and roughly chopped

25g black or green olives, pitted

salt and black pepper

Heat a tablespoon of the oil in a large flameproof casserole dish or a lidded frying pan. Season the chicken pieces with salt and pepper, then add a batch to the pan, skin-side down. Fry them for several minutes, until the skin is crisp and well browned, then turn them over and cook the underside for another few minutes. Remove from the pan and cook the rest in the same way, adding more oil if needed.

Add another tablespoon of oil to the pan and fry the onion and red pepper briskly over a medium heat, until they are starting to soften but are still al dente. Add the garlic and cook for a couple of minutes, then sprinkle in all the spices. Add the oregano and lemon zest, then stir until everything is well combined. Pour in the chicken stock and bring it to the boil, stirring constantly to scrape up anything stuck to the bottom of the pan.

Stir in the tomatoes, then put the chicken back in the pan, skin-side up. Partially cover the pan with a lid and cook the chicken over a low to medium heat for about half an hour. By this time it should be completely cooked through and tender. Remove the pan from the heat and stir in the olives. Check the seasoning, then leave the chicken to rest for a few minutes before serving.

To make the couscous, put the couscous in a bowl and pour over the orange juice and olive oil. Add the just-boiled water and cover the bowl. Leave the couscous to stand until all the liquid has been absorbed, then fluff it up with a fork. Stir the red onion and the herbs through the couscous. Sprinkle the chicken with the chopped herbs and serve it with the couscous.

Couscous

150g couscous

juice of 1 orange

2 tbsp olive oil

200ml just-boiled water

1 small red onion, finely
chopped

small bunch of flatleaf
parsley, leaves only

small bunch of mint,
leaves only

small bunch of coriander,
leaves only

To serve

1 tbsp chopped flatleaf
parsley

1 tbsp chopped mint

1 tbsp chopped coriander

MALLORCA AND MENORCA

Menorca and Mallorca are part of a little group of islands known as the Balearics and they're off the eastern coast of Spain. After all we'd heard about the influence of the Greeks, Moors and other conquerors in different parts of the Med, we were surprised to learn about the British in Menorca. The island was under British rule for much of the 18th century, and the first British governor was Richard Kane who did much to improve life there, building roads, schools and hospitals. The British sailors and soldiers brought gin – the popular drink at the time – to the island and wanted more, so the enterprising Menorcans began to distill it with great success. Gin is still produced in Menorca, and very good it is too, and this blending of Spanish and British cultures gave us the idea for our brilliant gin and tonic fish and chips.

In Mallorca we went to the market in Palma, one of the best we've ever been to. We bought some incredible almonds and then went on a trip to the island's almond groves where we met Rafa Nadal's nutritionist. She explained that the Mallorcan almonds are second to none, high in good fat and great food for athletes – if they're good enough for Rafa, they're good enough for us. We used almonds to make picada, a wonderful nutty sauce that's served with dishes like the lamb platillo. Much of the food on the islands is Catalan in style and we cooked and enjoyed dishes such as tumbet, Catalan flatbreads and black rice.

We were also lucky enough to eat at one of Palma's best restaurants, run by Marc Fosh who's a Brit. He cooked us great traditional Mallorcan food using local ingredients but with his own special twist and he was kind enough to give us one of his recipes for sea bass (see page 201).

CATALAN FLATBREADS

SERVES 4

Although definitely Catalan, these are like little veg-topped pizzas. They're known as coca Mallorquina and there are loads of versions, both savoury and sweet. The trick with our filling is to get the aubergine to absorb some liquid from the peppers while they rest. It stops them from drying out too much and burning when they are cooked on the flatbreads.

1 portion pizza dough
(see p.44)
extra flour, for dusting

Topping

1 large or 2 small
aubergines, sliced into
½cm rounds
6 tbsp olive oil
3 red peppers, deseeded
and cut in half
6 garlic cloves, skin on
1 tsp dried oregano
zest of 1 lemon
3 medium tomatoes
a few sprigs of oregano
or marjoram, leaves only
1 tbsp olive oil
salt and black pepper

Make the dough according to the instructions on page 44. While it is proving, make the topping. Preheat the oven to 180°C/Fan 160°C/Gas 4. Brush the aubergine slices with some of the oil and arrange them over a baking tray. Add the red peppers, skin-side up, and the garlic cloves. Drizzle a little olive oil over the peppers, then sprinkle everything with salt, pepper, dried oregano and lemon zest. Roast in the preheated oven for 30 minutes, until the pepper skin is slightly blackened and the aubergines are tender.

Tip the vegetables into a bowl and cover it with cling film. Leave them to steam until cool – the aubergines will take on the smoky flavour of the peppers. Peel the peppers and tear them into strips. Squash the flesh out of the garlic cloves and mash this into the remaining oil.

Thinly slice the tomatoes and sprinkle them with salt. Leave them to stand for about 10 minutes in a colander.

Turn the oven up to its highest setting. Knock back the dough and divide it in half, then place it on a floured surface and roll each piece into a long, slightly oval shape. Dust a couple of baking trays with flour and place the dough on them. Arrange the tomatoes on the dough, followed by the aubergines and peppers. Drizzle over the garlicky olive oil, then top with fresh oregano or marjoram leaves.

Put the flatbreads in the oven and turn the temperature down to 200°C/Fan 180°C/Gas 6. Bake the flatbreads for 20–25 minutes until the dough is cooked and the topping is tender. Serve at once.

PATATAS A LO POBRE

POOR MAN'S POTATOES

SERVES 4

To us, there's nothing poor about this. It's a comforting little one-pot that can be served as a tapa or it's great as a side dish with fish. It's often made with peppers but we like this version with fennel.

600g waxy potatoes, such as Charlottes

1 fennel bulb

75ml olive oil

2 garlic cloves, finely chopped

2 tbsp sherry vinegar

2 tbsp capers, rinsed

a few sprigs of fresh oregano

salt and black pepper

Slice the potatoes into 5mm-thick rounds. Don't bother to peel them – it adds to the charm of the dish and the flavour will be better. Trim the fennel, cut it into quarters lengthways then shred it into 5mm slices.

Heat the olive oil in a large, heavy-based pan and add the potatoes and fennel. Cook them over a medium heat for 10–15 minutes, until the potatoes are tender and starting to brown and crisp up around the edges. Keep turning the vegetables over very regularly and shaking the pan so everything falls into an even layer. After 10 minutes, start checking the potatoes with a knife tip to check if they are done.

When the potatoes are almost ready, add the garlic and sherry vinegar. Continue to cook for another 5–10 minutes until the liquid has been absorbed and the potatoes are completely cooked through. Stir in the capers and the oregano leaves, season with salt and pepper and serve immediately.

TUMBET

SERVES 4

A great Mediterranean veggie bake, this Mallorcan classic can be served on its own or with fish or meat. Traditionally all the vegetables are fried but we like to bake the aubergine slices, as they soak up less oil that way. We found waxy potatoes, like Charlottes, work best as they don't go soggy and it's fine to leave their skins on. It's really worth using fresh tomatoes for this, as they make the dish creamier and more mellow in flavour.

2 medium aubergines, cut into 1.5cm rounds

Up to 200ml olive oil

2 medium courgettes, cut into 2cm slices

500g large waxy potatoes (Charlottes), thinly sliced (about 3mm)

2 roast red peppers (see p.320), cut into strips

small bunch of fresh oregano

small bunch of fresh basil

salt and black pepper

Tomato sauce

2 tbsp olive oil

4 garlic cloves, crushed

400g ripe tomatoes, peeled and chopped

1 tsp dried thyme

pinch of sugar (optional)

Preheat the oven to 200°C/Fan 180°C/Gas 6. Arrange the aubergine slices on a large baking tray and brush them with some of the olive oil. Season them with salt and roast them in the oven for 20–25 minutes until softened and lightly browned. Remove and leave to cool.

Pour oil to a depth of ½cm into a large, heavy-based frying pan. Fry the courgettes over a medium heat for a couple of minutes on each side, then remove and drain them on kitchen paper. Season lightly with salt. Add the potato slices to the pan and fry them on both sides until they're softened all the way through and a light golden colour around the edges. This will take up to 10 minutes. Drain the potatoes on kitchen paper.

To make the sauce, put the olive oil in a saucepan and add the garlic. Cook for 3–4 minutes over a low to medium heat until the garlic is soft and you can smell its aroma, then add the tomatoes and thyme. Season with salt and pepper. Bring the sauce to the boil, then turn down the heat and cook it gently, uncovered, until well reduced – this will take about 25 minutes. Taste after 10 minutes and if the sauce tastes acidic, add a pinch of sugar.

Set the oven to 180°C/Fan 160°/Gas 4. Spread a couple of tablespoons of tomato sauce in the base of an oven dish. Sprinkle over some oregano and basil leaves, then top with the aubergine slices. Add more tomato sauce, then sprinkle with more herbs and add the courgettes. Repeat with more tomato sauce, herbs and the peppers, then finish with the last of the tomato sauce and herbs, and top with the potatoes. Season with salt and pepper and drizzle with a little more oil.

Bake the tumbet in the oven for 25–30 minutes until the potatoes are crisp and browned and the vegetables underneath are tender.

TORTILLA

WITH ASPARAGUS

SERVES 4

We've cooked lots of tortillas in our time, but we had to include this one in our Mediterranean selection. We love this asparagus version and we find that the thicker stems are best for this dish – they grill better and are easier to arrange than the longer thinner ones.

1 bunch of asparagus (about 250g)
3 tbsp olive oil
juice of ½ a lemon or lime
6 eggs
1 tsp dried mint or 1 tbsp finely chopped fresh mint
salt and black pepper

First prepare the asparagus – if using untrimmed asparagus, cut each one to about 20cm in length. Wash thoroughly and shake off any excess water. Don't bother to pat the asparagus dry, as it needs some liquid.

Heat a griddle or a frying pan until very hot. If using the griddle, toss the asparagus in a tablespoon of oil and lemon or lime juice, then season generously with salt and pepper. Griddle the asparagus for 2–3 minutes on each side until it is marked with char lines and is cooked but still has a bit of bite. Alternatively, heat the oil in a frying pan. Season the asparagus, add it to the pan and sear it for 2–3 minutes on each side. Set the asparagus aside.

Preheat your grill to its highest setting. Beat the eggs and season them with salt and pepper. Stir in the mint. Heat the remaining oil in a large frying pan, then pour in the eggs and arrange the asparagus on top. Leave the tortilla to cook for several minutes over a medium heat until the eggs have set and turned golden brown on the underside. Then, pop the frying pan under the hot grill and cook until the eggs have puffed up around the asparagus and have mostly set – a wobble here and there is good. Leave the tortilla to cool, then cut it into wedges to serve.

ARRÒS NEGRE

CATALAN BLACK RICE

SERVES 4

This is a favourite Catalan dish. You use ordinary paella rice and the black colour comes from squid ink, which you can buy in little sachets from your fishmonger. The chorizo provides lots of flavour so you don't need spices.

400g squid, cleaned

1 tbsp olive oil

200g cooking chorizo, diced

1 large onion, finely chopped

2 garlic cloves, chopped

4 medium tomatoes, peeled and diced

1.5 litres chicken, fish or vegetable stock

5 sachets of squid ink

500g paella rice

200ml white wine

salt and black pepper

To serve

4 tbsp roughly chopped flatleaf parsley,

1 portion of aioli (see p.162)

Rinse the squid well inside and out. Slice the body into rings and cut the tentacles in half if they're large.

Heat the olive oil in a large paella pan or a frying pan. Add the chorizo and sear it on all sides until well browned. Remove the chorizo from the pan with a slotted spoon and set it aside, then add the onion. Cook it for several minutes until translucent, then add the garlic and continue to cook for a couple of minutes. Turn up the heat, add the squid rings and the tentacles, and fry briskly until the squid turns opaque. Stir in the tomatoes and continue to cook, stirring constantly, until the tomatoes have broken down and any liquid has reduced.

Heat the stock in a saucepan and stir in the squid ink. Keep the pan over a low heat. Sprinkle the rice into the pan with the squid and tomatoes, then pour over the white wine. Leave the wine to simmer until most of it has evaporated, then make sure the rice is spread evenly across the pan and add all the stock. Season with salt and pepper.

Bring the stock to the boil, then turn the heat down and simmer gently until the rice is tender and the liquid has been absorbed into the rice. Stir regularly, just to make sure the rice isn't catching on the bottom of the pan. After 10 minutes, put the chorizo back in the pan and cook for another 5–10 minutes until the rice is tender and the liquid has been absorbed. Garnish with parsley and serve with a bowl of aioli on the side.

MARINATED SQUID

SERVES 4 AS A STARTER OR LIGHT MEAL

This is really good as it is, but if you want to make it a more substantial meal, add some veg such as fennel, new potatoes or green beans. You can also use cuttlefish for this recipe.

600g prepared squid, cut into rings

3 tbsp olive oil

juice and zest of 1 lemon

1 garlic clove, crushed

1 tbsp sherry vinegar

1 tsp sweet paprika

½ tsp hot paprika

small bunch of flatleaf parsley, chopped

a few sprigs of thyme

a few mint leaves

1 red onion, finely sliced into crescents

2 oranges, segmented (see p.320)

100g salad leaves, to serve

salt

Rinse the squid thoroughly inside and out. Bring a large saucepan of water to a fierce, rolling boil, then add salt. Add half the squid and cook it for 40 seconds exactly. Remove it with a slotted spoon and put it in a bowl of iced water. Bring the water back to the boil and cook the rest of the squid in the same way.

Put the olive oil, lemon juice and zest, garlic, sherry vinegar and paprikas into a bowl. Drain the squid thoroughly and add them to the bowl, then stir and cover. Leave them to chill in the fridge for at least an hour or overnight if you like.

Just before you are ready to serve, add the herbs and the red onion. Prepare the oranges as on page 320 and squeeze any juice out of the skin and membrane. Add the segments and juice to the squid and mix thoroughly. Serve immediately over salad leaves.

If you're using cuttlefish, you need one large prepared cuttlefish cut into strips. Cook it for 2–3 minutes – try a piece after 2 minutes for tenderness and cook for longer if necessary. Proceed as above.

GARLIC AND CHILLI PRAWNS

SERVES 4 AS A MAIN WITH BREAD AND SALAD OR 6–8 AS A STARTER

If, like us, you find it hard to get past this prawn dish when you see it on a menu, have a go and make your own. It's simple, it's sensational and bread to dip into the garlicky juices is a must. Use nice big juicy prawns and leave the tip of the tail and the head on – they look great that way.

600g whole king prawns (about 24 medium)

150ml olive oil

4 garlic cloves, very finely chopped

3 tbsp very finely chopped flatleaf parsley

generous pinch of chilli flakes

large pinch of sea salt

lemon wedges, to serve

Peel the prawns, leaving the tip of the tail and the head intact.

Pour the olive oil into a large frying pan and place it over a medium heat. Add the garlic, parsley, chilli flakes and salt, then cook for a couple of minutes, stirring constantly, until the garlic starts to soften but isn't taking on much colour.

Turn up the heat and add the prawns, frying them briskly on each side until they have turned pink all over. This will take 1–2 minutes on each side. Remove the prawns from the frying pan with a slotted spoon.

Serve them immediately with some of the flavoured cooking oil drizzled over the top, some lemon wedges on the side and some bread for dipping into the juices.

MARINATED MACKEREL

SERVES 4

This is a great dish for a dinner party as it can all be done a day ahead. The mackerel can take all the strong flavours, and the marinade turns this cheap, everyday fish into a glam Prince Charming. We love the taste of blood oranges but when they're not in season, just use regular oranges.

8 mackerel fillets

1 tbsp flour

75ml olive oil

3 garlic cloves, thinly sliced

1 onion, thinly sliced

2 bay leaves

2 strips of pared blood orange zest

2 strips of pared lemon zest

a few black peppercorns, lightly crushed

2 cloves

3cm cinnamon stick

generous pinch of chilli flakes or ½ tsp hot paprika

250ml blood orange juice

100ml fino sherry or white wine

50ml sherry vinegar

1 tsp honey

1 tsp salt

Dust the mackerel fillets in flour. Heat a tablespoon of olive oil in a large frying pan and fry the mackerel fillets, skin-side down, until almost all the flesh has turned an opaque white – this should take 3–4 minutes. Turn the fillets over – the skin should be crisp and browned – and fry them for a further minute. Remove the fillets from the pan and arrange them in an ovenproof dish.

To make the marinade, put the remaining olive oil in a saucepan. Add the garlic and sauté it briefly until it is just starting to colour, then remove it quickly with a slotted spoon. Don't leave the garlic unattended as it can burn and taint the flavour of the olive oil instead of flavouring it.

Add the slices of onion to the pan and cook them over a medium heat until starting to soften – you want the slices to keep their shape and still have a little bite, so cook them for no longer than 5 minutes. Add the bay leaves, orange and lemon zest, peppercorns, cloves, cinnamon stick and chilli flakes or paprika, then pour in the liquids. Finally, stir in the honey and season with a generous teaspoon of salt. Bring to the boil, then turn down the heat and simmer for 15 minutes.

Remove the marinade from the heat and leave it to cool. Pour the marinade over the fish – no need to strain it. Cover the dish and leave the fish to marinate overnight in the fridge. To serve, take the fish out of the fridge and allow them to return to room temperature. You can also heat them through in a low oven. Serve with some good hunks of bread or toasted baguette.

CUTTLEFISH OR SQUID STEW

SERVES 4

We found out all about the differences between cuttlefish, squid and octopus in a market in Menorca and we learned that they should either be cooked very quickly or very slowly. This stew is slow cooked and melts in your mouth. You can use squid if you can't find cuttlefish and frozen is fine too. Serve this with some bread to mop up the sauce or with new potatoes you can crush with your fork, or over pasta.

1 large cuttlefish, (about 1kg) or 1kg squid, cleaned

2 tbsp olive oil

1 large onion, finely chopped

3 garlic cloves, finely chopped

200ml white wine

400g tomatoes, skinned and chopped (fresh is best but you can use canned)

large sprig of thyme

2 bay leaves

1 tsp fennel seeds

a few basil leaves, to serve

salt and black pepper

Rinse the cuttlefish or squid inside and out. Cut the body into fairly thick slices and dry it as thoroughly as possible. Cut the tentacles in half if they're large.

Set a large flameproof casserole dish or a saucepan over a medium to high heat and add the olive oil. Add the cuttlefish or squid, and cook it quickly for 2–3 minutes until lightly coloured. Turn down the heat, then add the onion. Continue to cook, stirring regularly, for 10 minutes until the onion has softened. Add the garlic and cook for another few minutes.

Pour in the white wine and bring it to the boil. Let it bubble furiously for a couple of minutes, then add the tomatoes, herbs and fennel seeds. Season with salt and pepper. Cover the pan and simmer gently for about 1½ hours, until the cuttlefish or squid is tender.

Remove the lid and simmer the stew uncovered for another few minutes just to reduce the sauce slightly. Serve garnished with basil leaves.

FIDEUÀ

SEAFOOD AND NOODLES

SERVES 4

Fideu is a type of Spanish noodle used to make this Catalan super-soupy pasta and seafood dish, known as fideuà. If you can't find fideu noodles, use a fine 1mm vermicelli instead, but make sure it is a proper pasta vermicelli rather than a rice one. This is a fiesta in a bowl and a one-pot wonder.

12 large prawns, with heads and shells

3 tbsp olive oil

500ml fish stock

1 small onion, finely chopped

2 garlic cloves, finely chopped

200g squid, sliced into rings, tentacles left whole

4 medium tomatoes

1 tsp sweet paprika

pinch of saffron, ground with a pinch of salt

250g fideu, or broken-up vermicelli noodles

20 mussels or clams, cleaned

salt and black pepper

To serve

lemon wedges

aioli (optional – see page 162)

Shell the prawns and set the shells and meat aside separately. Heat a tablespoon of the oil in a large frying pan or a paella pan. Add the prawn heads and shells, and fry them until they've turned pink. Heat the fish stock in a separate saucepan, then add a ladleful to the prawn shells in the frying pan and let it bubble while you scrape up any sticky bits from the bottom of the pan. Simmer for 5 minutes, then strain the liquid into the saucepan of stock. Discard the prawn heads and shells.

Heat the remaining oil in the pan. Add the prawns and sear them on both sides very briefly, then remove them and set aside. Add the onion and cook them over a low heat for at least 10 minutes until soft and translucent. Turn up the heat, add the garlic and squid and fry for 2–3 minutes. Cut the tomatoes in half and coarsely grate them into the pan, then discard the skins. Add the paprika and saffron, then stir to combine.

Stir in the fideu noodles or the vermicelli. Mix very gently, then flatten the pasta out, making sure it is evenly spread over the base of the pan. Pour over the fish stock, then do not stir from this point on. Season with salt and pepper.

Bring the stock to the boil, pushing the pasta down so it is submerged. Add the mussels or clams, then turn down the heat and simmer until the pasta is just al dente, the shellfish have opened (discard any that don't) and much of the liquid has been absorbed. This shouldn't take any longer than 5 minutes.

Add the prawns, cover and cook for a minute, then remove the pan from the heat and leave to stand for 5 minutes. Serve with lemon wedges and aioli if you like.

FISH AND CHIPS

WITH GIN AND TONIC BATTER

SERVES 4

They make great gin in Menorca and that's what gave us this idea. It seemed daft at first but it really is fab. The gin makes a fresh crispy batter and the fizzy tonic adds sweetness and texture. When we do this, we like to par-fry the chips, then cook alternate batches of fish and chips until they're all done. You get stuck in the kitchen but you can serve everything hot. Pump up the gin if you like – just reduce the tonic accordingly. Lemon sole is good here as it keeps its shape, but any white fish that doesn't flake or break up would work.

500g skinned white fish fillets (such as lemon sole)

salt

Batter
200g plain flour

1 ½ tsp baking powder

generous pinch of salt

25ml gin

175ml tonic water

Chips
1kg potatoes (Maris Pipers or King Edwards)

vegetable oil, for frying

First make the batter. Put the flour into a bowl, then whisk in the baking powder and salt. Whisk in the gin and half the tonic water, whisking for as little a time as possible. It doesn't matter if the batter is slightly lumpy, it's more important that the mixture stays bubbly. Chill the batter for 30 minutes, then whisk in the remaining tonic water.

Next prepare the fish. Cut each fillet in half lengthways along the line of the backbone, then cut each piece on the diagonal into 3 long strips. Season them with salt.

Peel the potatoes and cut them into thick chips. Rinse them thoroughly for a couple of minutes to get rid of excess starch, then dry them as thoroughly as you can. Half fill a large saucepan with oil and heat to 160°C. Cook the chips in the oil until they are just cooked through but haven't taken on any colour. Remove them with a slotted spoon and drain them thoroughly on kitchen paper. If you have time, leave them to cool. Bring the oil up to 190°C, then cook the chips again until they are a deep golden brown. This should only take a couple of minutes.

To cook the fish, dip the strips into the batter. Heat the oil back to 190°C. Fry the fish in batches for 3–4 minutes. They will be done when they float to the top and have turned golden brown. Serve with the chips.

SEA BASS MALLORQUINA

SERVES 4

Marc Fosh has a Michelin-starred restaurant in Palma – and he's a Brit! We went on a tour of the Palma food market with him and then back to sample his Mediterranean fusion food at the restaurant. This was our favourite dish – sea bass served with soupy, saffrony potatoes – and he has very kindly shared the recipe with us. It's sensational.

olive oil

4 x 150g sea bass fillets

salt and black pepper

Vinaigrette

75ml sherry vinegar

30g sultanas

300ml olive oil

20g pine nuts, lightly toasted

300g tomatoes, peeled and diced

2 tbsp chopped flatleaf parsley

Warm potato, saffron and olive oil soup

100g roughly chopped onion

350g potatoes, peeled and quartered

800ml fish stock

pinch of saffron

300ml olive oil

To make the vinaigrette, bring the sherry vinegar to the boil in a small saucepan. Add the sultanas, then remove the pan from the heat. Set aside while the sultanas cool and absorb the vinegar. Once they are cool, toss them with the olive oil, pine nuts, diced tomatoes and parsley and season to taste. Set aside.

For the potato soup, put the onion, potatoes and fish stock in a saucepan and bring to the boil. Add a pinch of saffron, then simmer for 15 minutes until the potatoes are cooked. Remove the pan from the heat, add the olive oil and blend in a food processor. Pass the mixture through a fine sieve and keep it warm.

Heat a little olive oil in a heavy-based frying pan. Season the fish fillets with salt and pepper. When the oil is hot, add the fillets, skin-side down, and cook them for 1–2 minutes until the skin is golden and crispy. Turn them over and cook for another 2–3 minutes.

Place each fillet in a large bowl and spoon some vinaigrette on top. Pour some warm potato, saffron and olive oil soup around the outside and serve.

SALT COD SALAD

SERVES 4

Salt cod isn't cheap but this tasty refreshing recipe helps a little go a long way. Most people think of salt cod being in fritters or in a paste, but this is a serious savoury salad, bouncing with citrus and chillies. Although the eggs are traditional with this kind of salt cod dish, the salad is great with or without them so it's up to you.

250g salt cod
2 bay leaves
1 garlic clove, thinly sliced
a few peppercorns
½ tsp fennel seeds
1 piece of thinly pared lemon zest

Salad
½ red onion, finely sliced
1 celery stick, diced
½ green pepper, diced
1 chilli, deseeded and finely diced
1–2 little gems, shredded
2 medium tomatoes
1 orange
2 tbsp finely chopped flatleaf parsley or basil
2 eggs, hard-boiled and cut into quarters (optional)

Dressing
juice from the orange
2 tbsp olive oil
juice of 1 lemon
¼ tsp hot paprika
salt and black pepper

First soak the cod – you will need to start this a full day ahead. Put the cod in a large container and cover it with cold water. Leave it to soak at room temperature for 24 hours, changing the water at least 4 times.

Drain the cod and put it in a saucepan. Cover with fresh water and bring it to the boil, then simmer for 5 minutes and drain. Repeat this process. Put the cod back in the pan and cover it with fresh water. Add the bay leaves, garlic, peppercorns, fennel seeds and lemon zest. Heat gently until the water is almost boiling, then turn the heat down and leave the cod to simmer for 10 minutes. Remove the pan from the heat and leave the fish to cool in the water. Meanwhile, put the red onion slices to soak in a bowl of salted water for 30 minutes to remove any bitterness.

Put the drained onion slices, celery, green pepper, chilli and lettuce in a large serving bowl or on a platter. Cut the tomatoes in half, discard the core and seeds, and dice the flesh finely, then add it to the salad. Peel and segment the orange as on page 320, collecting any juice in a bowl. Cut each segment into 3 pieces and squeeze the juice from the discarded peel and membrane.

To make the dressing, whisk the reserved orange juice with the rest of the ingredients. Add plenty of salt and pepper.

Shred the salt cod, discarding any skin or bones, then put it in the serving bowl. Add the herbs, then pour over the dressing. Toss very gently and garnish with the egg quarters, if using.

SAFFRON-BRAISED CHICKEN

WITH PICADA

SERVES 4

This is as good as it sounds. The marinade bathes the chicken in flavour and the picada – a fab mix of almonds and breadcrumbs spiced up with sherry and chilli – gives the dish body and takes it to another dimension. Bravo!

4 chicken legs
1 tbsp olive oil
1 large onion, thickly sliced
1 garlic clove, chopped
200ml white wine
200ml chicken stock

Marinade
3 tbsp olive oil
grated zest and juice of 1 lemon
large pinch of saffron
½ tsp cinnamon
2 garlic cloves, crushed
2 bay leaves, crumbled
salt and black pepper

Almond picada
2 tbsp almonds
1 tbsp olive oil
25g breadcrumbs
25ml white wine or fino sherry

First, mix all the marinade ingredients together and season. Pour the marinade over the chicken and massage it in, getting under the skin where possible. Put the chicken in a bowl and chill it for at least an hour in the fridge, but preferably overnight.

For the picada, lightly toast the almonds in a dry frying pan until you smell their delicious aroma. Remove the pan from the heat and leave the almonds aside to cool. Heat the oil in the same frying pan, add the breadcrumbs and fry them until they have soaked up the oil and turned a rich golden brown. Remove the pan from the heat and pour the white wine or sherry over the crumbs. Put the nuts in a food processor and grind until they are the texture of very fine breadcrumbs. Add the fried breadcrumbs, chilli, garlic and parsley and continue to process until the sauce is completely smooth – add a little water or stock if need be. Set it aside.

Remove the chicken from the fridge and let it come up to room temperature. Brush off any excess marinade. Heat the tablespoon of oil in a large, heavy-based frying pan and sear the chicken legs, skin-side down, until the skin is well browned and crisp. This will take several minutes. Turn the legs over and brown the other side.

Remove the chicken from the pan and add the onion. Cook it for 5 minutes over a medium heat until it's just starting to soften, then add the garlic and cook for a further 2 minutes. Pour in the white wine, bring to the boil and cook until reduced by about half, then add the stock and the picada.

pinch of chilli flakes
1 garlic clove, finely chopped
2 tbsp finely chopped flatleaf parsley

To serve
2 tbsp finely chopped flatleaf parsley

Stir thoroughly, then place the chicken legs, skin-side up, into the pan. Bring the liquid back to the boil, then turn down the heat to a simmer and partially cover the pan. Cook for a further 20 minutes or until the chicken is tender and cooked through, and the sauce has reduced. If the sauce is reducing too much, turn down the heat and add a splash of water. Serve sprinkled with parsley.

BLACK PUDDING

WITH ONIONS

SERVES 4

Black pudding, morcilla or boudin noir – we love it all. This is good served on toasted bread as part of a tapas feast or it makes a great starter or tasty brunch. Spanish black pudding is called morcilla but it's fine to use regular British black pudding and we find that it's easier to slice than morcilla. We've included some of the spices you get in morcilla in this recipe to give that real Moorish flavour.

2 tbsp olive oil

1 large onion, sliced into crescents

2 garlic cloves, finely chopped

1 tsp dried oregano

1 tsp sweet paprika

½ tsp hot paprika

½ tsp ground allspice

½ tsp cumin

pinch of cloves

pinch of cinnamon

250g black pudding, peeled and diced

2 tomatoes, deseeded and diced

salt and black pepper

To serve

thin slices of baguette

2 tbsp finely chopped flatleaf parsley

Heat half the olive oil in a large frying pan. Add the onion and fry it gently for about 10 minutes until soft and translucent. Add the garlic, oregano and all the spices and cook for a couple more minutes, then season with salt and pepper. Add 100ml of water and leave everything to simmer for a couple of minutes.

In a separate frying pan, heat the remaining olive oil. Add the black pudding and fry it briskly on all sides until crisp. Then gently toss the black pudding with the onion mixture and the tomatoes.

Toast the bread, pile the black pudding mixture on top and serve garnished with chopped parsley.

BRAISED RABBIT

WITH ARTICHOKES AND WHITE WINE

SERVES 4–6

Rabbit is a popular meat in Mallorca and Menorca and this is a good way to cook it – a nice easy one-pot. Rabbit is lean and can be dry if you're not careful so we've used quite a bit of oil in this to compensate and keep everything lovely and juicy. And to make life easy we use grilled artichokes from a jar or from the deli counter.

4 tbsp olive oil

2 onions, finely sliced

6 garlic cloves, finely chopped

1 red chilli, finely chopped or 1 tsp hot paprika

1 rabbit, cut into 6 pieces, or 6 rabbit legs

1 piece of pared lemon zest

300ml fino sherry or white wine

2–3 sprigs fresh of oregano, leaves only, finely chopped

6 grilled artichokes, cut in half

salt and black pepper

To serve

2 tbsp finely chopped flatleaf parsley

1 garlic clove, finely chopped

zest of ½ lemon

Heat the olive oil in a large lidded frying pan or a flameproof casserole dish. Add the onions, partially cover the pan and cook them over a low heat for 10–15 minutes until they are very soft and translucent. Stir regularly. Add the garlic and the chilli or paprika and cook for a few more minutes.

Turn up the heat and add the rabbit pieces. Continue to cook until the rabbit has taken on some colour on each side and the onions have started to brown. Season with salt and pepper. Tuck in the lemon zest and pour over the sherry or wine.

Bring to the boil, then turn down the heat and leave the rabbit to simmer, partially covered, for 20–25 minutes. Add the oregano and artichokes and continue to cook, uncovered, for a further 10 minutes, until the sauce is slightly syrupy and the rabbit is tender.

Mix the parsley, garlic and lemon zest in a bowl. Serve the rabbit and artichokes sprinkled with the parsley mixture.

PORK OR LAMB SKEWERS

SERVES 4

You can't beat a kebab and these are laced with fab Moorish spices. If you like, you could use the North African spice mixture called ras el hanout, which often features in Spanish tapas dishes, instead of all the individual ones. You'd need about a tablespoon.

600g pork or lamb, diced
lemon wedges, to serve
salt and black pepper

Marinade

2 tbsp olive oil
juice of ½ lemon
(or a Seville orange
when in season)
1 tbsp sherry vinegar
2 garlic cloves, crushed
1 tsp cumin
1 tsp ground coriander
½ tsp cinnamon
¼ tsp cayenne
¼ tsp turmeric
1 sprig of rosemary,
leaves only, finely
chopped
1 tsp dried mint

Season the pork or lamb with salt and pepper. Mix all the marinade ingredients together in a bowl and add the meat. Mix everything thoroughly, then cover the bowl and leave the meat in the fridge to marinate for at least 2 hours, but preferably overnight.

Remove the meat from the fridge a good half an hour before you want to cook it so it can come up to room temperature. Soak 8 wooden or bamboo skewers for half an hour to stop them burning – or use metal ones. Thread the pieces of lamb or pork on to the skewers.

Prepare the barbecue and heat until the coals are white or heat a griddle on the hob until it is too hot to hold your hand over. Cook the skewers, turning them regularly. For medium rare lamb, cook for 7–8 minutes, but cook the pork for longer and check it is cooked right through.

Leave the skewers to rest for 5 minutes before serving with lemon wedges and some salad.

LAMB PLATILLO
WITH GREEN PEAS
SERVES 4

A celebration of lamb and peas, this dish can be made with lamb chops but we like to use lamb neck fillet which is cheaper and dead tasty. One thing to mention – it's important to cook the peas until they're very soft. They won't look so pretty and green but they taste really nice and sweet and that's the way the Spanish like them. The lamb is served with another version of picada, which delivers that final explosion of flavour.

2 tbsp olive oil

750g lamb neck fillet, cut into thick chunks

1 tbsp flour

2 onions, finely chopped

4 medium tomatoes, peeled and finely chopped

½ tsp cinnamon

1 tsp dried oregano

2 bay leaves

sprig of thyme

500g fresh or frozen peas

salt and black pepper

Picada

1 tbsp almonds

1 tbsp hazelnuts

1 tbsp olive oil

25g breadcrumbs

25ml dry sherry (optional, can use water instead)

pinch of saffron

pinch of chilli flakes

2 garlic cloves, finely chopped

small bunch of flatleaf parsley, leaves only

Heat a tablespoon of the oil in a flameproof casserole dish. Season the lamb and dust it with flour, then fry it in batches, making sure it's all seared and well browned on all sides. Set the browned lamb aside.

Add the remaining oil to the pan. Add the onions and fry them over a medium heat until translucent and starting to caramelise – this will take at least 10–15 minutes. Add the tomatoes, cinnamon and herbs. Continue to fry over a low to medium heat for 5 minutes until the tomatoes have broken down and have given up any excess liquid.

Put the lamb back in the pan and stir to coat it with the onions and tomatoes. Pour over just enough water to cover, then bring to the boil. Turn down the heat to a simmer, then cover the pan and cook the lamb for about an hour, until it is tender. Add the peas, then cover and simmer for another 15 minutes.

Meanwhile, make the picada. Toast the nuts in a dry frying pan until they're lightly coloured and aromatic, then remove them and set them aside to cool. Heat the oil in the pan, add the breadcrumbs and fry them until they have soaked up all the oil and have turned a rich golden brown. Remove the pan from the heat and pour over the sherry or water. Mix the saffron with a pinch of salt and grind it to a powder using a pestle and mortar.

Transfer the nuts to a food processor and grind them to a fine powder. Add all the remaining ingredients and continue to process until the mixture is completely smooth – it should not be at all grainy. If necessary, ladle off a little liquid from the pan and add it to the picada a tablespoon at a time while the motor is running. This should help loosen the mixture and make it easier to get a smooth sauce. Add the sauce to the pan and simmer, this time uncovered, for another 15 minutes. Serve immediately.

MALLORCAN SPICED PORK

SERVES 6–8

Mallorcan cooking is rich in great pork dishes and we cooked this roast for the programme. The pork skin is scored – ask your butcher to do that for you – then rubbed with all these wonderful herbs and spices. It's perfect served just with the aromatic pan juices or you can add wine or sherry and some flour to make a gravy. And if you fancy a change, put some sliced fennel instead of onions in the roasting tin.

2–2.5kg boned
pork shoulder, rolled,
skin scored
1 tbsp olive oil
juice of ½ lemon
2 onions, thickly sliced

Rub

4 garlic cloves, crushed
1 red chilli,
finely chopped
1 tbsp fennel seeds,
lightly crushed
4 cloves, ground
½ tsp black peppercorns,
crushed
1 tsp smoked paprika
1 tsp cinnamon
1 tsp dried thyme
1 tsp dried oregano
3 tbsp olive oil
1 tbsp sherry vinegar
salt

Gravy (optional)

1 tbsp plain flour
100ml white wine
or fino sherry

Preheat the oven to 230°C/Fan 210°C/Gas 8. Mix all the rub ingredients, including the oil and vinegar, together and season well with salt. Push the rub into the score lines of the pork skin and deep into the flesh – you should be able to do this without cutting through the meat as the joint is rolled. Wipe off any excess, then rub the pork with the tablespoon of olive oil and pour over the lemon juice. Sprinkle the skin with salt.

Spread the onion over the base of a roasting tin and place the pork on top. Add 250ml of water. Roast the pork at the high heat for half an hour by which time the skin should be starting to crisp up and brown. Reduce the heat to 180°C/Fan 160°C/Gas 4, then continue roasting for another 25 minutes per 500g of meat – so if you have 2kg joint, cook it for another hour and 40 minutes.

Remove the pork from the oven and leave it to rest, lightly covered with foil, for at least 15 minutes. Strain off the contents of the roasting tin, arranging the onions around the pork if you like, then wait for the liquid to settle. Skim off the fat (there will be quite a lot).

If making gravy, sprinkle a tablespoon of flour over the roasting tin and stir well over a medium heat until you have scraped up anything stuck to the base of the tin. Add the wine or sherry and mix until you have a roux-like paste. Add the skimmed pan juices and thin with a little more water if necessary to make a gravy.

Alternatively, simply serve the pork with the skimmed pan juices – they will have plenty of flavour from the rub.

SOUTHERN SPAIN

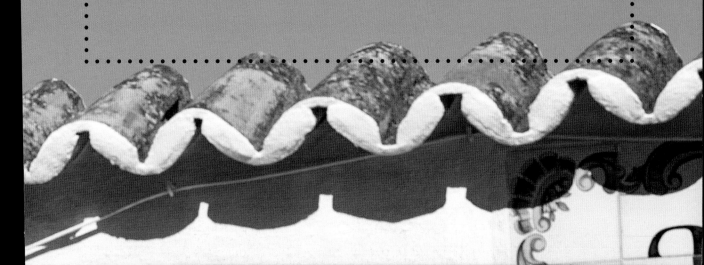

For the final leg of our journey we travelled down the Mediterranean coast of Spain from Valencia to Torremolinos. It was an action-packed trip – we learned flamenco dancing, went to some mud baths to make ourselves beautiful and along the way sampled some great food. We met three lovely ladies who revealed the mysteries of paella to us. Basically every region has its own recipe, which is the best of course, and it can be as local and specific as your particular valley. The ladies cooked us their excellent paella which contained rabbit, belly pork and cherries and we then made our own rabbit and snail version. We also tried our hand at making a proper gazpacho and discovered that there is white gazpacho made with almonds as well as the classic tomato. It was superb.

The far south of Spain is closer to Africa than the rest of Europe and there are definitely lots of North African and Moorish influences on the food; plenty of paprika and other spices. We got heavily into tapas – those little plates of delicious morsels you get offered in Spanish bars – and found them such a great way of eating. And we decided that a tapas feast would be the perfect way to end our trip – a wonderful mishmash of everything Mediterranean. On the night of 23 June people celebrate the festival of San Juan to mark the summer solstice and there are beach parties and bonfires all along the coast of Spain. We were invited along and took some of our tapas dishes – mushrooms with garlic and sherry vinegar, garlic and chilli prawns, black pudding with onions, and padron peppers – to the party to share with everyone. It was the best night and we knew we would be back in the Mediterranean sometime soon.

SPICED CARROTS

SERVES 4 OR MORE WITH OTHER TAPAS

This reminds us of a carrot salad we did in Morocco years ago and it really deserves a place on our tapas table. Simple but tasty.

400g medium carrots (8–10), trimmed

2 tbsp olive oil

1 garlic clove

1 tsp grated orange zest

1 tsp coriander seeds, crushed

½ tsp cumin seeds

½ tsp ground ginger (optional)

150ml chicken or vegetable stock (or water)

a few coriander leaves

a few mint leaves

salt

Cut each carrot into 4–6 pieces, depending on their thickness, lengthways. If the carrots are more cylindrical than conical in shape, make the cuts on the diagonal to ensure each piece is pointed.

Heat the olive oil in a large, lidded frying pan, add the carrots and season them with salt. Cover the pan and cook the carrots over a high heat for 7–8 minutes, shaking the pan regularly, until they are starting to soften and caramelise.

Add the garlic, orange zest, coriander and cumin seeds and the ginger, if using. Cook, uncovered, for another 2–3 minutes. Pour over the stock or water and continue to cook for a few more minutes until the sauce is reduced and the carrots are just cooked through – they should be quite firm.

Serve garnished with the fresh coriander and mint.

MUSHROOMS

WITH GARLIC AND SHERRY VINEGAR

SERVES 4 OR MORE WITH OTHER TAPAS

These garlicky mushrooms are a popular tapas dish in Spain and they make a good starter too. You can make this with white, button or crimini mushrooms, but it's best with a selection – chestnuts, portobellini, oyster and so on – or you could get one of the fancy boxes of mixed mushrooms you see in the supermarkets these days. We served this at the festival of San Juan on a beach in Torremolinos. Olé!

2 tbsp olive oil

4 garlic cloves, finely sliced

500g mushrooms, larger ones halved or sliced

2 tbsp sherry vinegar

salt and black pepper

To serve

drizzle of olive oil

pinch of hot paprika

small bunch of flatleaf parsley or fresh coriander, chopped

Heat the olive oil in a large frying pan. Add the garlic and fry it for 1 minute, stirring constantly. Add the mushrooms and sauté them over a high heat until just browned. If they are cooked on a high enough heat they should not give out any liquid, but if they do, continue to cook until the pan is dry.

Season with salt and pepper, then pour in 2 tablespoons of the vinegar. It should sizzle in the pan, then continue to cook until most of the liquid has evaporated.

Serve with another drizzle of olive oil, a light sprinkling of paprika and plenty of chopped parsley or coriander.

BROAD BEANS
WITH HAM AND MINT
SERVES 4 OR MORE WITH OTHER TAPAS

Broad beans are everywhere in the Med – sometimes just plonked on the table still in their pods as a snack with an aperitif. This recipe is great for lunch with a slab of crusty bread and a glass of red wine, or as part of a tapas spread. If you like you could use some diced chorizo or morcilla (Spanish black pudding) instead of ham. Removing the skins from the beans is a labour of love but makes all the difference, we promise you.

600g broad beans, freshly podded or frozen (about 1.5kg if in pods)

2 tbsp olive oil

4 spring onions, sliced into rounds

75g Serrano ham, finely diced

2 garlic cloves, finely chopped

50ml sherry (something robust such as a sweeter Oloroso or Amontillado)

small bunch of mint leaves

salt and black pepper

Bring a saucepan of salted water to the boil, then add the broad beans. Blanch them for 2 minutes, then drain and run them under cold water to cool. Slip off the greyish skin from each one to reveal the bright green bean underneath.

Heat the olive oil in a large pan. Add the spring onions and cook them for a couple of minutes. Add the ham and garlic and continue to cook gently – the aim is to soften both, not to crisp them up and brown.

Add the broad beans and season with salt and pepper, then turn up the heat. Pour in the sherry and allow to bubble up for 30 seconds, then add 50ml of water. Simmer for a minute – the liquid should look syrupy and reduced. Tip everything into a serving dish and sprinkle with the mint leaves. This is nice served warm or at room temperature.

ROAST RED PEPPERS

WITH TOMATOES AND CUMIN

SERVES 4 OR MORE WITH OTHER TAPAS

A tasty tapas dish, this is moreish as well as Moorish! You could also make it with aubergines, cut into long strips, brushed with oil and roasted for about 30 minutes until browned. And an alternative garnish could be capers and green olives.

4 red peppers, cut in half, deseeded and stems removed

3 tbsp olive oil

1 tsp cumin seeds

4 garlic cloves, skins on

100g ripe tomatoes, skinned

pinch of sugar (optional)

finely grated zest of ½ lemon

small bunch of oregano, parsley or basil leaves

salt and black pepper

Preheat the oven to 200°C/Fan 180°C/Gas 6. Place the peppers skin-side up on a baking tray and drizzle them with a tablespoon of the olive oil. Put the peppers in the oven and roast for 15 minutes. Take the tray out, turn the peppers over and add the cumin seeds and garlic. Reduce the oven temperature to 180°C/Fan 160°C/Gas 4 (you can leave the door open for a couple of minutes to help it drop more quickly), then roast for another 30 minutes until softened.

Put the peppers and garlic cloves in a plastic bag or in a covered bowl and leave them to cool to room temperature. Once the peppers are cool, peel off their skins and pull them into thick strips. Arrange the strips on a serving platter.

Squeeze the garlic flesh out of the skins, put it in a blender or food processor with the tomatoes and blitz to make a sauce. Season with salt and pepper, and taste – add a little sugar if the tomatoes aren't sweet enough. Blitz again, drizzling in the remaining 2 tablespoons of olive oil.

Sprinkle over the lemon zest and the herbs and serve the peppers at room temperature with the sauce.

BRAISED PEAS

WITH ARTICHOKES

SERVES 4 OR MORE WITH OTHER TAPAS

This is a good side dish, great with white fish and popular all over the Mediterranean area. We use the grilled artichokes you get in jars but you can use frozen or fresh if you don't mind the fiddle of getting to the hearts. If you do use fresh artichokes, blanch them first, then cook them on a griddle.

1 tbsp olive oil

15g butter

1 shallot, finely chopped

4 large grilled artichoke hearts, cut into quarters

300g peas, fresh or frozen

salt and black pepper

To serve

1 tbsp finely chopped mint leaves

1 tbsp finely chopped flatleaf parsley leaves

Heat the olive oil and butter in a lidded frying pan or a saucepan. When the butter starts to foam, add the shallot and fry it gently for a few minutes until it starts to turn translucent. If you're using artichokes that haven't already been grilled, turn up the heat and add them to the pan, then sear them on the cut sides. Otherwise, leave the heat fairly low and add the artichokes and the peas at the same time. Season with salt and pepper, then pour over 150ml of water.

Bring to the boil and cover the pan. Turn down the heat and simmer for 10 minutes, until the peas are very tender and the liquid has reduced. Serve sprinkled with the finely chopped mint and parsley leaves.

PADRON PEPPERS

SERVES 4 OR MORE WITH OTHER TAPAS

You can get these Spanish favourites in our supermarkets now and they're the beer snack everyone loves. There's loads of vitamin C in peppers so they're good for you too. We like to fry them in some veg oil and save the good extra virgin stuff for drizzling over the top before we tuck in.

1 tbsp vegetable oil
150g padron peppers
2 tbsp extra virgin olive oil
flaked sea salt

Heat the vegetable oil in a large, preferably cast-iron, frying pan. When the air above the oil starts to shimmer and the pan is too hot to hold your hand over comfortably, add the padron peppers.

Cook them on one side for just a minute, which is how long it should take for the skin to start to blacken and blister, then turn them over. Cook for another minute, then continue to cook, shaking the pan regularly, for another 2–3 minutes until the peppers are blistered all over and have softened to the point that they are just tender.

Remove the peppers from the pan and drizzle over the oil. Sprinkle with a generous pinch of flaky sea salt and serve immediately while hot or at room temperature.

CHICKPEAS AND SPINACH

SERVES 4 OR MORE WITH OTHER TAPAS

They love their chickpeas in Spain and this dish makes a great supper as well a good addition to a tapas feast. You can use canned chickpeas but it's easy to soak and cook the dried ones and they do taste even better. Cook up a whole batch and stash them away in the freezer.

1 tbsp olive oil

500g spinach

300g cooked or canned chickpeas (see p.317)

salt and black pepper

Sauce

3 tbsp olive oil

50g white bread, cut into cubes

25g flaked almonds

3 garlic cloves, sliced

1 tsp sweet paprika

1 tsp ground cumin

pinch of cayenne

1 tbsp red wine vinegar

First make the sauce. Heat the 3 tablespoons of olive oil in a frying pan, add the bread and fry it briskly over a medium heat until the cubes are light golden brown on all sides. Add the almonds and garlic and continue to cook until the almonds are also lightly coloured. Tip the contents of the frying pan into a bowl and set it aside to cool.

Transfer the bread, almonds and garlic to a food processor. Add the paprika, cumin and cayenne and season with plenty of salt and pepper, then pulse until the mixture resembles fine breadcrumbs. Remove a tablespoon of the mixture and set it aside. Drizzle the vinegar and 100ml of water into the food processor and continue to process until you have a runny paste – it doesn't have to be completely smooth. Alternatively, you can make the sauce using a large pestle and mortar.

For the chickpeas and spinach, heat the tablespoon of oil in a large flameproof casserole dish or a saucepan. Shred and wash the spinach, but don't drain it too thoroughly – you need some of the water that clings to the leaves for the cooking process. Gradually add the spinach to the pan, pushing it down until it has all wilted. Add the cooked or canned chickpeas and the sauce, then stir to combine. Season with salt and black pepper.

Simmer, uncovered, for 5 minutes, stirring regularly. Sprinkle with the reserved bread and almond mixture, then serve.

WHITE BEANS
IN SPICY SAUCE
SERVES 4 OR MORE WITH OTHER TAPAS

All over the Mediterranean, people love their pulses and no tapas selection is complete without some beans. Speaking as lovers of British canned beans, we have to admit that this Med version of beans on toast is a lot more tasty.

500g cooked Spanish white beans (see p.317 or from a jar)

4 tbsp olive oil

1 small onion, finely chopped

2 garlic cloves, finely chopped

small sprig of thyme, leaves only

1 tbsp tomato purée

1 tsp smoked paprika

1 tbsp sherry vinegar

3 tbsp finely chopped flatleaf parsley

salt and black pepper

To serve (optional)

slices of rustic, country-style bread, toasted

½ garlic clove

olive oil

a few pickled anchovies, to garnish (optional)

Drain the white beans, reserving 100ml of their cooking or preserving liquid. Heat the olive oil in a frying pan. Add the onion and fry it gently until it is very soft and slightly caramelised. Add the garlic and thyme leaves and continue to cook for a couple more minutes.

Add the tomato purée and stir until the mixture starts to separate, then stir in the smoked paprika, sherry vinegar and the reserved liquid. Season with salt and pepper. Bring to the boil, then turn the heat down and simmer for 3–4 minutes just to give the flavours a chance to meld together. Stir in the beans – the sauce should just coat them, leaving them glossy with the oil and paprika. Sprinkle with parsley.

Serve the beans as part of a tapas selection or on toasted bread rubbed with garlic and drizzled with olive oil. Add the anchovies, if using, criss-crossing them over the beans.

PATATAS BRAVAS

SPICY POTATOES

SERVES 4

Patatas bravas can be served as a tapa or with a main course and they're awesome. They're often drenched in tomato sauce but we like this spicy version with lots of paprika and no tomatoes. The potatoes stay nice and crisp this way too. You can fry the potatoes with loads of oil or roast them in the oven – whichever you fancy. Great served with the meatballs on page 258.

800g floury potatoes, peeled and cut into 3–4cm chunks

200ml olive oil (or 2 tbsp, if roasting)

2 tbsp finely chopped flatleaf parsley, to serve

salt

Sauce

2 tbsp olive oil

2 garlic cloves, finely chopped

1 tbsp sherry vinegar

½ tsp sugar or honey

1 tbsp sweet paprika, plus extra to serve

1 tsp hot paprika, plus extra to serve

Put the potatoes in a saucepan and cover them with cold water. Bring them to the boil and add plenty of salt, then simmer for 3–4 minutes until they are starting to soften. Drain carefully.

To fry the potatoes, heat the olive oil in a large frying pan. Add the potatoes in a single layer and fry them until crisp and brown on all sides – this will take 15–20 minutes to do properly. You may need to cook the potatoes in more than one batch if you can't fit them all in; it's best not to overcrowd the pan.

To roast the potatoes, preheat the oven to 200°C/Fan 180°C/Gas 6. Put just 2 tablespoons of oil in a roasting tin and heat it in the oven. Add the drained potatoes, toss them in the oil, and roast for 40–45 minutes.

To make the sauce, heat the olive oil in a small saucepan and add the garlic. Cook for 2–3 minutes until the garlic has started to soften but hasn't taken on any colour. Add the vinegar and the sugar or honey and stir until dissolved. Finally stir in the sweet and hot paprikas.

Pour the sauce over the crisp potatoes and sprinkle with a little extra of both the sweet and hot paprikas. Garnish with a little finely chopped parsley.

EMPANADILLAS

SPANISH PATTIES

MAKES 12

The empanada has babies! These mini versions are just right as snacks with drinks or to pop in your lunchbox. Make them by the dozen and your friends will love you for it. We like to use tuna from a jar for these.

Pastry

250g plain flour

½ tsp baking powder

generous pinch of salt

50ml olive oil, plus extra for oiling

50ml fino sherry or white wine

up to 50ml iced water

Filling

25g golden raisins

pinch of saffron

1 tbsp olive oil

½ red onion, finely chopped

½ red pepper, diced

1 celery stick, finely chopped

1 garlic clove, finely chopped

1 tbsp tomato purée

50ml white wine or sherry

25g green pitted olives, thinly sliced

25g capers

zest of ½ lemon

a few parsley leaves, finely chopped

200g flaked tuna

olive oil, for brushing

First make the pastry. Put the flour and baking powder in a bowl with a generous pinch of salt. Mix the olive oil and the sherry or wine together, make a well in the centre of the flour and gradually work in the oil and wine. Add up to 50ml of iced water to form a dough. Turn the dough out on to a lightly oiled work surface (you don't want to work more flour in) and knead until the dough is smooth and elastic. Wrap it in cling film and chill in the fridge for at least half an hour.

To make the filling, put the raisins and saffron in a small bowl and add enough just-boiled water to cover the raisins. Leave them to stand. Heat the oil in a frying pan and add the onion, pepper and celery and sauté for about 10 minutes until the onion is soft and translucent. Add the garlic and cook for another minute or so, then stir in the tomato purée and wine. Mix thoroughly and cook over a low heat for 4–5 minutes, then stir in the olives, capers and lemon zest, then the raisins, saffron and soaking water. Simmer until the liquid has reduced and the mixture is quite dry, then stir in the parsley and the tuna. Remove from the heat and leave to cool.

Preheat the oven to 200°C/Fan 180°C/Gas 6. Roll the dough out on a floured work surface. Be firm with it as it is very elastic and it will take some working before it stops springing back. When the dough is very thin (1–2mm), cut out 12 x 10cm diameter rounds, re-rolling it as necessary.

Place dessertspoonfuls of the mixture on half of each round, making sure you leave a border. Dampen the edges with water, then stretch the uncovered half over the filling and seal. Crimp around the edges with a fork, then brush the pastry with olive oil.

Arrange the empanadillas on a baking tray and bake in the oven for 20–25 minutes until the pastry is crisp and golden brown and the pasties are slightly puffed up.

SALT COD CROQUETAS

MAKES 16

Viva this much-abused tapas bar treat. Everyone loves a croqueta and we find they disappear like wildfire. If you want more croquetas – and we wouldn't blame you – double the amount of salt cod, potato, onion, celery and parsley. We like these served with a bowl of good mayonnaise – see our recipe on page 312.

100g salt cod
600ml milk
1 bay leaf
1 sprig of oregano
1 sprig of thyme
200g potatoes (peeled weight), cut into fairly small chunks
1 tbsp olive oil
½ small onion, very finely chopped
½ celery stick, very finely chopped
2 garlic cloves, finely chopped
2 tbsp finely chopped flatleaf parsley
½ tsp hot paprika or chilli powder (optional)
vegetable oil, for deep-frying
lemon wedges
salt and black pepper

To coat
50g plain flour
2 eggs, beaten
50g fine breadcrumbs

First soak the cod – you will need to start this a full day ahead. Put the cod in a large container and cover it with cold water. Leave it to soak at room temperature for 24 hours, changing the water at least 4 times.

Break up the cod and put it in a saucepan. Cover it with the milk and add the herbs. Bring the milk to the boil, then turn down the heat and simmer for 20 minutes. Add the potatoes and continue to cook for about 10 minutes until they are tender. Remove the potatoes from the pan with a slotted spoon, put them in a bowl and add a couple of tablespoons of the milk. Mash them roughly with a fork and season to taste. Drain the fish, discarding the remaining milk and the aromatics. Flake the fish and add it to the mash, discarding any skin and bones.

Heat the olive oil in a frying pan and add the onion and celery. Sauté until soft and translucent, then add the garlic and cook for a couple more minutes. Remove the pan from the heat and allow the contents to cool, then add to the potatoes and fish along with the parsley and the paprika or chilli powder, if using, and mix thoroughly. Make sure the mixture is at room temperature, then chill it for an hour.

To coat the croquetas, put the flour, eggs and breadcrumbs in 3 separate bowls. Dip each croqueta in the flour, then pat off the excess, coat thoroughly in egg, then press it into the breadcrumbs. Make sure they are completely covered.

Half fill a large saucepan or a deep-fat fryer with vegetable oil and heat to 180°C. Add the croquetas, a few at a time, and cook them for 3–4 minutes, flipping them over once or twice, until they are deep golden brown. Drain on kitchen paper and serve with lemon wedges.

GAZPACHO

SERVES 4-6

You can't go wrong with a good gazpacho – the most refreshing thing on a hot sunny day. Everyone thinks this is packed with garlic but in fact we learned that you only need one clove and a little raw garlic goes a long way. The garnishes are important so set them all out and let everyone put together their own bowlful.

1 large red pepper

1 large green pepper

100ml extra virgin olive oil

1kg tomatoes, skinned

1 large cucumber (about 600g), peeled and deseeded

1 garlic clove, finely chopped

75g stale white bread

1 tbsp red wine vinegar

salt and black pepper

Garnishes

2 hard-boiled eggs

50g olives, finely chopped

50g can of anchovies (30g drained weight), finely chopped

50g cucumber, finely diced

a few mint leaves, chopped

a few flatleaf parsley leaves, chopped

Preheat the oven to 200°C/Fan 180°C/Gas 6. Cut the peppers in half, cut out the cores and any large white membrane and brush off the seeds. Place the peppers cut-side down on a baking tray and drizzle them with a little of the olive oil. Roast them for half an hour, until the skin has started to blacken, then put them in a bowl and cover. Leave the peppers to steam and cool down. When they are cool enough to handle, peel off the skins.

Put the peppers, tomatoes and cucumber into a blender or food processor. Add the chopped garlic. Roughly tear up the bread and add this along with the rest of the olive oil and the red wine vinegar. Season with salt and pepper.

Blitz until very smooth – you can push everything through a sieve to make sure it is completely smooth if you like. Tip the soup into a bowl and chill it in the fridge. When you are ready to serve the soup, stir it thoroughly, then taste and adjust the flavour with more red wine vinegar and seasoning. Check the texture – it should be the right consistency for soup, but add a little cold water to thin it if necessary.

Separate the egg whites and yolks and chop both finely. Put them in small bowls. Put all the other garnishes into small bowls for serving at the table with the gazpacho so everyone can help themselves.

PATAQUETAS

MAKES 12

These crescent-shaped breads are traditional in the Valencia region and date back to the 17th century. They're a bit like Italian ciabatta – lovely and crusty on the outside and soft inside and we couldn't eat them quick enough. The name means 'little hoof' which makes sense when you look at the shape.

Starter/ferment
100g plain flour
7g instant yeast
1 tsp sugar
100ml tepid water

Dough
500g strong white bread flour, plus extra for dusting
250ml tepid water
1 tsp salt
oil, for greasing

Mix the starter ingredients in a bowl to make a sticky, fairly thick dough. Leave it for 15 minutes just to give the yeast a kick start, then cover the bowl with cling film and put it in the fridge for at least 24 hours, preferably for 48 hours.

When you are ready to make the bread, remove the starter dough from the fridge and allow it to return to room temperature before using. It should be spongy with large, visible air bubbles on the surface and throughout the dough. Transfer it to a large bowl or the bowl of a stand mixer, then mix in the strong white bread flour, water and salt. The dough will be sticky to start with. Either turn the dough out on to a floured work surface and knead it for 10–15 minutes, or knead it with a dough hook in the stand mixer for at least 5 minutes, until the dough is smooth and elastic. Divide the dough into 12 pieces and roll them into balls. Place these on a lightly oiled baking tray and cover them with a damp cloth. Leave to stand for 20 minutes.

To shape, take each ball, put it on a floured surface and press it down lightly into a flat disc – it should be about 10cm in diameter. Make a cut from the centre of the disk, downwards, through to the edge, then prise the 2 sides apart, pinching in the tips as you go, so the dough is crescent shaped. Make a further cut horizontally across the dough, just above the first cut, but this time just score without cutting right through – look at the picture and you'll see what we mean. Place the crescents well spaced out on baking trays.

Cover them with a damp cloth or oiled cling film and leave them somewhere warm to rise. They should double in size and spring back when pressed with a finger.

Preheat the oven to 200°C/Fan 180°C/Gas 6. Boil a kettle and pour the water into a deep roasting tin. Put this in the bottom of the oven. Dust the crescents with flour, then place them in the oven. Bake for about 25 minutes, until the rolls are golden brown and sound hollow when tapped.

AJO BLANCO

WHITE GAZPACHO

SERVES 4-6

Gazpacho isn't only cold tomato soup. This Moorish version is amazing – creamy and fragrant without too strong a hit of garlic. Peeling the grapes really does make a difference so think of Mae West and get to it!

200g whole blanched almonds

75g white bread, crusts removed

600ml iced water

2 garlic cloves, finely chopped

½ cucumber, peeled and deseeded, roughly chopped

75ml olive oil

1–2 tbsp sherry vinegar or white wine vinegar

salt and black or white pepper

To garnish

1 tbsp flaked almonds

24 seedless green grapes, peeled and halved

2 tbsp olive oil

Put the almonds in a dry frying pan and toast them over a medium heat. Shake the pan regularly and watch it very closely. Remove the pan from the heat as soon as you can smell the almonds and they are just starting to take on some colour. Toast the flaked almonds for the garnish in the same way and set them aside.

Cover the bread with some of the iced water and soak it for 10 minutes until softened. Drain and squeeze out the excess water.

Put the whole almonds in a food processor or a blender. Add the soaked bread and process until the almonds are fairly finely ground. Add the garlic and cucumber and continue to blitz, then drizzle in the rest of the iced water, the oil and half the vinegar. Taste, season with salt and pepper, then drizzle in a little more vinegar if you think it needs it. The soup should be very smooth but if it seems grainy, push it through a fine sieve. Transfer it to a bowl or jug, cover and chill for 2 hours.

To serve, ladle the soup into bowls and top with peeled grapes, toasted flaked almonds and a drizzle of olive oil.

CHORIZO AND CHESTNUT SOUP

SERVES 4

Chorizo sausage and chestnuts crop up in loads of recipes in southern Spain and we loved this rich, spicy soup. Don't forget – it's not always hot in the Med and sometimes you need a nice winter warmer. This is a big flamenco of a soup!

2 tbsp olive oil

2 red onions, finely chopped

2 mild cooking chorizo, skinned and finely diced

1 hot cooking chorizo, skinned and finely diced

3 garlic cloves, finely chopped

1 tsp dried oregano

1 tsp dried thyme

1 tsp ground cumin

400g can of tomatoes

250g cooked chestnuts (vacuum packed are fine), crumbled

800ml chicken stock

pinch of sugar (optional)

small bunch of flatleaf parsley, chopped, to serve

salt and black pepper

Heat the olive oil in a large saucepan. Add the onions and fry them over a medium heat for 10–15 minutes until soft and slightly caramelised. Reserve a tablespoon of the mild chorizo and a teaspoon of the hot chorizo for the garnish, then add the remainder to the onions. Continue to cook for a few minutes until the chorizo is lightly browned and some of the fat has rendered out.

Add the garlic, herbs and cumin, then cook, stirring continuously, for another 2–3 minutes. Add the tomatoes, chestnuts and chicken stock and season with salt and pepper. Bring the soup to the boil, then taste – if it is slightly acidic from the tomatoes, add a pinch of sugar.

Simmer the soup for 10 minutes. Remove the pan from the heat and give the soup a few blasts with a stick blender until almost smooth – leave some texture.

Fry the remaining chorizo until crisp and brown. Serve the soup sprinkled with the chorizo and freshly chopped parsley.

HAKE

WITH ROMESCO SAUCE

SERVES 4

We don't eat enough hake in this country. Our mums would just poach it in milk but it's an amazing fish and in Spain it's a star. Serve it with this romesco sauce which has more balls than a matador. Good with some patatas bravas (see page 232) too.

4 hake fillets, skin on
1 tbsp flour
1 tbsp olive oil
lemon wedges, to serve
salt and black pepper

Romesco sauce
2 tomatoes, halved
1 red pepper
6 garlic cloves, skin on
100ml olive oil
75g breadcrumbs
(from sourdough or
robust white bread)
1 tbsp blanched almonds
1 tbsp blanched hazelnuts
1 tbsp red wine vinegar
2 tsp smoked paprika
a few sprigs of flatleaf
parsley

First make the sauce. Preheat the oven to 200°C/Fan 180°C/Gas 6. Put the tomatoes, red pepper and garlic in a roasting tin and roast them for about 25 minutes until the tomato and pepper skin is slightly blackened and the garlic is tender. Remove the tin from the oven and cover it with foil, so the veg continue to steam as they cool down. When they're cool enough to handle, peel the tomatoes, pepper and garlic cloves.

Heat about a tablespoon of the olive oil in a frying pan and add the breadcrumbs. Fry for a few minutes until the breadcrumbs are lightly brown, then tip the crumbs on to a plate to cool down. Wipe out the frying pan, add the almonds and hazelnuts and toast them until they are a light golden brown.

Put the almonds and hazelnuts into a food processor and grind them until they resemble fine breadcrumbs. Add the peeled tomato, pepper and garlic along with the breadcrumbs, vinegar, paprika and parsley. Season with salt and pepper. Blitz briefly to combine, then with the motor still running, drizzle in the remaining oil. Continue to process until the sauce is completely smooth – it should not be at all grainy. Taste and add more seasoning, paprika and vinegar if necessary. Leave the sauce to stand.

To fry the hake, dust the fillets with flour and season them on both sides with salt and pepper. Add the olive oil to a large frying pan and when it's hot, add the hake fillets, skin-side down. Fry them for about 4 minutes, until you can see that the skin is very crisp around the edges and the fish is very nearly completely opaque. Flip them over and cook on the other side for a minute only. Serve the hake with the sauce and lemon wedges for squeezing over at the table.

GRILLED SARDINES

SERVES 4

Sardines vary a lot in size so it's hard to say how many to get. Also some people will eat only a couple, while others will want loads. Fortunately they're very cheap so err on the generous side and everyone will be happy. And when sardines are done well there's nothing better. Cook them filleted or whole – we grilled ours on a barbecue on the beach. And if you're worried about grilling fish, you can fry them instead.

16–20 fresh sardines, whole or filleted

olive oil

Marinade

50ml olive oil

1 tbsp sherry vinegar

juice and zest of 1 lemon

4 garlic cloves, crushed

1 tsp sweet smoked paprika

½ tsp cayenne or hot paprika

small bunch of fresh oregano or marjoram, leaves only, finely chopped

lemon wedges, to serve

salt and black pepper

Mix the marinade ingredients together and add plenty of salt and pepper. If using whole sardines, cut a couple of slashes on each side. Add the sardines to the marinade and turn them over, making sure they are completely covered. Leave them for half an hour – no longer than that or they will start to cook in the marinade.

When you are ready to cook the sardines, heat a griddle pan or a heavy-based frying pan until very hot. Brush it with a little olive oil. Drain the sardines from the marinade, scraping off the excess and reserving anything left in the bowl.

If using fillets, add them to the pan skin-side down – you may have to cook them in a couple of batches. Press them down with the back of a fish slice or spatula to stop them curling up too much. Cook for 3–4 minutes. You will know when the fillets are ready to turn over as they will be crisp around the edges and they should come away from the pan easily without sticking. Leave for a minute longer if they are reluctant. Cook on the flesh side for another couple of minutes, then remove. If using whole sardines, cook them for 3–4 minutes on each side on the griddle or in the frying pan.

If you have fried the sardines, add the marinade to the pan to heat through briefly once you've removed the sardines. If using a griddle pan, heat the marinade in a small saucepan. Serve the sardines with the marinade on the side for spooning over them, and with lemon wedges.

BRAISED CHICKEN
WITH CHORIZO AND PEPPERS
SERVES 4

A Spanish one-pot with classic Med flavours – who could ask for more? Be sure to use cooking chorizo and there's lots of flavour in the spicy fat that oozes out. We like to add some chickpeas or white beans near the end of the cooking time or you could serve it with super-tasty baby potatoes roasted with garlic.

1 tbsp olive oil

4 chicken legs or 8 chicken thighs, skin on, bone in

150g cooking chorizo (picante or dulce, to taste), sliced

1 large onion, cut into thin wedges

1 red pepper, cut into thick strips

1 green pepper, cut into thick strips

2 garlic cloves, finely chopped

1 tsp sweet smoked paprika

½ tsp hot paprika (optional)

1 tsp dried sage

1 tsp dried oregano

200ml white wine

400g can of chickpeas or beans, drained (optional)

salt and black pepper

Heat the olive oil in a large heavy-based frying pan that has a lid. Season the chicken pieces with salt, then add them to the pan, skin-side down, and sear until they are well browned on all sides. Don't be tempted to skimp on this stage – it should take at least 10 minutes.

Remove the chicken from the pan and add the chorizo. Sear it quickly on both sides, then remove it from the pan. Add the onion and peppers and sauté them for 10 minutes over a medium heat until they're softening around the edges but still with a bit of bite. Add the garlic, paprikas and dried herbs and stir to combine.

Put the chorizo back in the pan and pour over the wine. Add the browned chicken and bring to the boil. Turn the heat down, partially cover the pan, and simmer everything gently for 20–25 minutes until the chicken is completely cooked through. Add chickpeas or beans, if using, for the last 10 minutes or so of the cooking time.

Serve the chicken with the chorizo, vegetables and sauce.

GRILLED CHICKEN

SERVES 4

This is similar to Italian devilled chicken (the one with lots of black pepper), but with a Spanish touch in the marinade. It's good served with some aioli (see page 162) on the side if you fancy.

1 chicken, cut into 8 pieces, or 8 thighs or drumsticks
lemon wedges, to serve

Marinade
50ml olive oil
4 garlic cloves, crushed
4 bay leaves
1 tsp dried oregano
1 tsp chilli flakes
1 tsp black peppercorns, lightly crushed
100ml fino sherry
salt

Mix all the marinade ingredients together in a bowl and add plenty of salt. Add the chicken pieces and rub the marinade in thoroughly, getting under the skin as well where possible. Cover and leave the chicken in the fridge for at least 3 hours, but overnight if you can.

Remove the chicken from the fridge an hour before you want to cook it so it can come up to room temperature. Brush off the marinade and reserve it. Get your barbecue going and when the coals are white hot, push them into the middle. Place the chicken pieces around the edges of the grill so they will cook on indirect heat to start with. Cover the barbecue with the lid and cook the chicken for 30 minutes, turning regularly. Move the chicken over the direct heat to crisp up and continue to cook for another 15–20 minutes until it is cooked through and nicely charred on the outside. Baste regularly with the reserved marinade.

If you don't want to grill the chicken over coals, cook it under the grill or in a griddle pan. Heat the grill to its highest setting or heat a griddle pan until it is too hot to hold your hand over. Grill the chicken pieces for 10–15 minutes on each side, basting them regularly with the marinade, until they are cooked through (check by piercing the thickest part with a skewer – the juices should run clear) and the skin is crisp and brown.

Serve with lemon wedges and a green salad or a veg dish such as patatas a lo pobre (poor man's potatoes – see page 180).

WHITE BEANS
WITH CHORIZO AND GREENS
SERVES 4

We know this is a very simple dish, but the sauce is rich and gutsy and we honestly don't think it needs anything else. Those jars of Spanish white beans are good for this and use dulce or picante chorizo, depending on whether you want heat or not. Serve with crusty bread and a big fat smile.

2 tbsp olive oil

200g cooking chorizo

2 red onions, cut into wedges

2 garlic cloves, finely chopped

100ml red wine

500g cooked white beans, well rinsed, (from a jar or see p.317)

1 tsp dried oregano

2 bay leaves

300ml chicken stock

200g cavolo nero or similar, thickly shredded

salt and black pepper

Pour the olive oil into a large saucepan or flameproof casserole dish and put it over a high heat. Add the chorizo and sear it briefly on both sides, then turn the heat down to medium and add the onions. Cook them for several minutes until they are starting to colour but are still firm, then add the garlic and cook for a couple of minutes more. Turn up the heat again and pour in the wine. Let it bubble for a couple of minutes until it has reduced by half, then add the white beans.

Sprinkle in the oregano and tuck in the bay leaves. Season with salt and pepper. Stir so everything is well combined, then pour over the chicken stock. Bring the stock to the boil, then turn down the heat and leave everything to simmer for 10 minutes. Add the cavolo nero, sitting it on top of the beans. Cover the pan and cook until the greens have wilted down and are cooked through – you want the stems to be tender to the point of a knife. This will take 15–20 minutes.

Stir the greens into the rest of the ingredients. The dish should be soupy with quite a thick sauce. Serve it in large bowls with some bread to mop up the juices.

CHICKEN SKEWERS

WITH OREGANO

SERVES 4

They love a barbecue in the Mediterranean but so do we in the UK. You can cook this on a griddle indoors, but they are seriously good cooked over wood or charcoal. A perfectly balanced kebab – no chilli sauce required!

8 boneless, skinless chicken thighs

1 red pepper, cut into 3cm squares

1 green pepper, cut into 3cm squares

lemon wedges, to serve

Marinade

2 tbsp olive oil

zest and juice of 1 lemon

1 tsp honey

1 tbsp dried oregano

1 tbsp sweet smoked paprika

½ tsp cinnamon

salt and black pepper

Cut each of the chicken thighs into 4 pieces, trimming off any large pieces of fat as you do so.

For the marinade, put the olive oil, lemon zest and juice and the honey in a bowl and whisk to dissolve the honey. Add the oregano, paprika and cinnamon, as well as a generous amount of salt and black pepper. Mix thoroughly. Add the chicken and stir to make sure it is completely covered with the marinade. Cover and leave it in the fridge for at least 3 hours. You can leave it overnight if you like.

Half an hour before you are ready to cook the chicken, remove it from the fridge so it can come back to room temperature. Soak 8 wooden or bamboo skewers in water for half an hour. Thread the chicken pieces on to the skewers, alternating them with squares of pepper.

Prepare a barbecue or heat a griddle until very hot. Grill the chicken skewers for 15–20 minutes, turning them regularly, until the chicken and peppers are cooked through and nicely charred in places. Baste the skewers once or twice with the leftover marinade as they cook. Serve with lemon wedges.

RABBIT PAELLA

SERVES 6

Everyone knows about paella but we'd never had this rabbit and snails version, which is a real classic apparently. We like to keep the rabbit on the bone but you can use rabbit (or chicken) off the bone if you prefer. Canned snails are fine here – and you can leave them out if you're not a fan. Do feel free to change whatever ingredients you wish. The truly authentic paella can be specific to the very valley that you live in. In Spain we cooked one with rabbit, pork and cherries!

300g fresh large tomatoes

1 tbsp olive oil

1 rabbit or chicken, jointed into 10 pieces

4 garlic cloves, crushed

1 tsp saffron threads, soaked in a little warm water

1 tsp sweet smoked paprika

zest of 1 lemon

1.5 litres hot chicken stock

3 bay leaves

2 sprigs of thyme

200g green beans, cut into short lengths

150g cooked white or haricot beans (can use canned)

100g broad beans (skinned if large)

500g paella rice

12 snails, cooked (optional)

lemon wedges, to serve

salt and black pepper

Cut the tomatoes in half, remove the seeds and grate the flesh, then set aside. Discard the skins. Heat the olive oil in a large paella pan or frying pan. Add the rabbit or chicken pieces and fry them until well browned, then remove them from the pan and set aside.

Add the garlic and cook for a further couple of minutes. Add the grated tomato flesh and the saffron in its soaking water, then fry for a few more minutes. Stir well and sprinkle in the paprika and lemon zest. Put the rabbit or chicken back in the pan. Pour in all but a large ladleful of the hot chicken stock and sprinkle in the bay leaves, thyme, green beans, white or haricot beans and the broad beans and season with a little salt and pepper.

Bring the chicken stock to the boil, then sprinkle in the rice, stirring gently to make sure it is spread as evenly as possible. This is the only time you should stir the paella. Bring the liquid back to the boil and cook for 5 minutes.

Turn the heat down and leave the rice to simmer slowly until cooked – this should take 12–15 minutes. If the pan is getting dry, taste the rice and if it's still too crunchy, add a little more stock and continue to cook. When you are satisfied the rice is al dente, arrange the snails, if using, over the paella.

Take the pan off the heat and cover it with a damp tea towel or a lid. Leave the paella to stand for 10 minutes, so the rice can finish cooking and the snails can cook through. Serve with lemon wedges.

ALBONDIGAS

SPICY MEATBALLS

SERVES 4-6

The Moors ruled much of Spain for centuries and had a big influence on the cooking, introducing loads of spices and other ingredients. We've made our meatballs with lamb but you can use beef or pork instead or a mix of all three. These are fab served with patatas bravas (see page 232). In the UK it's usually easiest to make a good sauce with canned toms, but if you have some lovely Mediterranean fresh tomatoes, use those and it will be even better.

600g minced lamb

2 garlic cloves, crushed

1 tbsp ground coriander

2 tbsp ground cumin

1 tsp sweet paprika

½ tsp ground cinnamon

1 tsp ground cardamom

small bunch of flatleaf parsley, finely chopped

zest of 1 lemon

100g breadcrumbs

50ml double cream

1 egg

3-4 tbsp olive oil

salt and black pepper

Tomato sauce

2 tbsp olive oil

1 onion, finely chopped

2 garlic cloves

½ tsp cinnamon

½ tsp cayenne

½ tsp cumin

½ tsp turmeric

2 bay leaves

400g can of tomatoes

1 tsp honey

100ml yoghurt (optional)

To serve

3 tbsp finely chopped flatleaf parsley leaves

To make the meatballs, put all the ingredients, except the olive oil, into a large bowl. Season with plenty of salt and pepper and mix thoroughly with your hands. The mixture will feel wet to start with, but as you mix and knead it, it will stiffen up. Shape the mixture into balls of about 50g – you should end up with about 16.

To fry the meatballs, heat the oil in a large frying pan and fry the meatballs until well browned on all sides – do this in a couple of batches. Alternatively, preheat the oven to 200°C/Fan 180°C/Gas 6. Put the meatballs on an oiled baking tray, and cook them for about 15 minutes until well browned and just cooked through. Keep them warm.

To make the sauce, heat the oil in a saucepan. Add the onion and sauté for about 10 minutes until it's softened and translucent. Add the garlic, spices and bay leaves and cook for another couple of minutes, stirring constantly, then add the tomatoes and honey. Pour over 200ml of water and bring to the boil. Turn down the heat, cover the pan and leave the sauce to simmer for 15 minutes. Remove the lid and simmer for another 5 minutes, then stir in the yoghurt, if using.

To finish the dish, put the meatballs into a large, deep frying pan, and cover them with the sauce. Simmer gently for 5 minutes until the meatballs have heated through and the sauce has reduced a little. Serve sprinkled with freshly chopped parsley.

DESSERTS

In many of the places we visited, pudding was simply a perfectly ripe peach, a few figs and a piece of cheese, or a bowl of beautifully sweet cherries. What more could you want? But there are also plenty of great Mediterranean dessert and cake recipes and we decided to put them together in one chapter.

People tend to eat the heavier desserts in the winter months and some are associated with particular celebrations or festivals. Many showcase fruit and we visited some fruit growers near the French town of Céret, close to the border with Spain. Christine and Fabrice specialise in growing cherries and apricots and shared some of their delicious jam with us. In turn, we made fabulous cherry meringues and an apricot and almond tart. Oranges, too, are grown all over the Mediterranean area and we used them in an orange and almond cake and an orange flan as well as a wonderful sorbet.

We've also included some excellent traditional recipes such as the Catalan Swiss roll known as bras de gitan (or arm of the gypsy), Mallorcan ensaïmada pastries, zabaglione and crema Catalana. And we've given a few old favourites a special Mediterranean twist, such as our bread and butter pud glammed up with Pedro Ximénez sherry and – would you believe it? – a Nutella ice cream!

ENSAÏMADAS
MALLORCAN SPIRAL PASTRIES
MAKES 16

They make huge versions of these pastries in Mallorca, but we think these small ones are easier to cope with. Traditionally, they're stuffed with lard but we've used a lovely almond paste instead. We like a drop of orange blossom water as well, but that's up to you. We ate some gourmet ones stuffed with foie gras – a guilty pleasure but they were fabulous.

500g plain flour, plus extra for dusting

150g caster sugar

7g dried yeast

pinch of salt

200ml milk

2 eggs, beaten

oil, for greasing

icing sugar, for dusting

Almond filling

100g caster sugar

100g softened butter

100g ground almonds

a few drops of almond extract

a few drops of orange blossom water (optional)

First make the dough. Put the flour, caster sugar and yeast into the bowl of a stand mixer with a pinch of salt and mix to combine. Heat the milk until just tepid, then mix it with the eggs. With the motor running, gradually add the milk and eggs until you have a tacky, smooth dough. Knead it with a dough hook until the dough is soft and smooth and no longer sticky. Transfer it to an oiled bowl and cover it with a damp tea towel, then leave the dough to rise for a couple of hours until doubled in size. Alternatively, you can make the dough by hand, then turn out it out on to a lightly floured surface and knead until it is smooth. Leave it to rise as before.

For the filling, beat the sugar and butter together until soft and fluffy. Add the ground almonds, almond extract and orange blossom water, if using, then set aside.

Transfer the dough to a lightly floured work surface and divide it into 16 pieces. Keep the pieces covered with a damp tea towel until you're ready to use them. Shape each piece of dough into a ball, then roll it out to about 15–20cm in diameter. Add a dessertspoon of the filling mixture and spread it out with a spatula, leaving a small border all the way round. Roll the dough up tightly, then roll or massage it into a long sausage about 25cm long. Roll this into a coil, like a snail shell, tucking the outside end underneath. Make sure you do this quite loosely, otherwise the middle coils will not have enough space to spread and will push upwards. Repeat with the remaining dough and filling.

Place the ensaïmadas on a couple of baking trays and cover them with a damp tea towel. Leave them to rise for another hour or so until doubled in size again. Preheat the oven to 180°C/Fan 160°C/Gas 4. Bake the ensaïmadas for about 12 minutes until lightly golden and cooked through. Leave them to cool, then sprinkle with icing sugar before serving.

BRAS DE GITAN

CATALAN SWISS ROLL

SERVES 6-8

In southern France, near the border with Spain, we met Christine and Fabrice who grow wonderful cherries and apricots in their orchards near Céret. We cooked some great jam with them and then used it to make this traditional cake, which is like a Catalan version of a Swiss roll. It's just what you need after a hard day picking fruit.

Sponge

50g plain flour
50g ground almonds
1 tsp baking powder
pinch of salt
4 large eggs
75g caster sugar
a few drops of almond extract
1 tbsp Grand Marnier or other eau de vie
2 tbsp caster sugar, for dusting

Crème patissière

300ml milk
vanilla pod, split
2 egg yolks
65g caster sugar
40g cornflour
1 tbsp Grand Marnier or other eau de vie
a few drops of almond extract

First make the crème patissière. Pour the milk into a saucepan and add the vanilla pod. Bring the milk to the boil, then remove the pan from the heat and leave the milk to infuse until it's back to room temperature.

Put the egg yolks and sugar in a bowl and whisk until well combined and starting to turn pale, then whisk in the cornflour. Reheat the milk, then transfer it to a jug, discarding the vanilla pod. Rinse out the saucepan. Pour the milk into the egg and sugar mixture from a height, whisking constantly, then tip it back into the saucepan. Add the alcohol and the almond extract, then stir over a low to medium heat until thickened. Transfer it to a bowl and cover with cling film, making sure the cling film sits on top of the surface of the crème patissière to stop it from forming a skin. When the mixture has cooled down, put it in the fridge to chill.

Preheat the oven to 180°C/Fan 160°C/Gas 4. Line a 30 x 20cm Swiss roll tin with baking paper.

For the sponge, sift the flour, ground almonds and baking powder into a bowl. Add a pinch of salt. Whisk the eggs and sugar together in a separate bowl with an electric hand whisk until the mixture is pale with an aerated, mousse-like texture – if you pull the whisk across the mixture it should leave a ribbon trail. Add the almond extract and the Grand Marnier or other eau de vie.

Add the flour and almond mixture to the bowl with the eggs and sugar and fold in very gently but thoroughly with a metal spoon. Pour the mixture into the prepared tin and spread with a palette knife to make sure it is even. Bake for 10–12 minutes until lightly browned and springy to the touch. Remove the sponge from the oven and turn it out on to a rack. Peel off the baking parchment and leave to cool.

To serve

4 tbsp cherry or apricot jam (see pp.300–301)

2 tbsp icing sugar

3 tbsp flaked almonds, lightly toasted

To assemble, transfer the sponge to a lightly moistened tea towel. Spread over the jam, then top with the crème patissière. Spread it evenly with a palette knife, leaving a wide (at least 5cm) border along the top (the filling will spill over otherwise) and a narrower one (2cm) on each side.

Carefully roll the sponge up from the bottom, pulling it up and over to try to stop the filling falling out. Don't worry if the sponge cracks a little. Sprinkle with icing sugar and the toasted almonds.

FIG BISCOTTI

MAKES ABOUT 30

We northerners love a fig roll with a cup of tea and this is a sophisticated Italian figgy treat – crunchy biscuits just right for dipping into an espresso coffee or a glass of sweet wine. We've used the trad method of baking them twice for real crispness. They keep well too if you can resist them.

275g plain flour
1 tsp baking powder
200g caster sugar
grated zest of 1 orange
pinch of salt
100g hazelnuts, halved
100g dried figs, chopped into about 8 pieces
2 eggs
1–2 tbsp orange juice or orange blossom water

Preheat the oven to 180°C/Fan 160°C/Gas 4. Line 2 baking trays with some baking paper.

Put the flour, baking powder, sugar and orange zest in a bowl and add a pinch of salt. Whisk to get rid of any lumps, making sure the zest isn't clumping together, then stir in the hazelnuts and figs. Make a well in the centre and add the eggs, then mix to make a fairly dry dough. Add a tablespoon of the orange juice or orange blossom water, then if the dough is still too dry, add more, a little at a time, until you have a smooth dough.

Divide the dough into 2 pieces and roll each into a round log of about 5cm in diameter – each log should be at least 20cm long. Place the logs on the prepared baking trays and flatten them very slightly.

Bake the logs in the preheated oven for 25–30 minutes, until they have spread slightly, are lightly golden brown around the edges and firm to the touch. Remove them from the oven.

Reduce the oven temperature to 150°C/Fan 130°C/Gas 2. When the logs are cool enough to handle, cut them into slices – you can do this on the diagonal. You should get 15–18 pieces from each log. Spread the biscotti over the 2 baking trays, leaving plenty of space between them. Put them back in the oven for another 20 minutes, turning them over half way through the cooking time.

Remove the biscotti from the oven. They will continue to crisp up as they cool. Once the biscuits are cool, store them in an airtight container. They will keep for at least a week.

CANESTRELLI BISCUITS

MAKES ABOUT 48

These crunchy little biscuits are found all over Italy and are popular in Corsica too. Like a lot of Mediterranean recipes, they have travelled. We've flavoured these with aniseed but you could use lemon or orange zest instead if you like. They're just the thing with your espresso.

250g plain flour, plus extra for dusting

1 tsp baking powder

pinch of salt

1 tbsp aniseed, lightly crushed

75g caster sugar

50ml olive oil

75ml white wine

1 tbsp pastis such as Pernod (optional)

Preheat the oven to 180°C/Fan 160°C/Gas 4. Sieve the flour and baking powder into a bowl, add a large pinch of salt, then stir in the aniseed and the caster sugar. Mix the olive oil, white wine and pastis, if using, together. Make a well in the centre of the flour mixture and pour in the wet ingredients, stirring as you go, until the dough comes together. Knead the dough very lightly until it's smooth.

Dust your work surface with flour and roll or press out the dough until it is about 1cm thick. Cut the dough into 2.5cm thick slices, then cut each slice into diamonds. You should end up with about 48 small biscuits. Arrange these on a baking tray – they can be crammed together so one tray should be enough. Bake them for 15 minutes until puffed up slightly and starting to colour. Turn the heat down to 160°C/Fan 140°C/Gas 3 and cook the biscuits for a further 10–15 minutes until they are light golden brown in colour. They will still feel slightly soft in the centre but will firm up as they cool.

Leave the biscuits to cool on the baking tray, then transfer them to an airtight container. They will keep for up to a month.

CREMA CATALANA

SERVES 6

This is like crème brûlée but lighter and not as rich, so easier on the tum. We had a wonderful one in Sardinia, where we had our first whiff of Catalan food in a town called Alghero, which was ruled by the Catalans in the Middle Ages. Street names there are still shown in Catalan as well as in Italian.

500ml whole milk
300ml double cream
zest of 1 lemon
zest of ½ orange
1 cinnamon stick
6 egg yolks
100g caster sugar
2 tbsp cornflour

Topping
6 tbsp caster sugar

Put the milk and double cream in a saucepan with the citrus zests and cinnamon stick. Bring the milk and cream almost to the boil, then remove the pan from the heat, cover and leave the mixture to infuse as it cools.

Put the egg yolks and caster sugar in a bowl and beat with an electric hand-held whisk until the mixture is well aerated with a pale, mousse-like texture. Sift the cornflour into the bowl and whisk it in until completely combined.

Reheat the milk, again almost to boiling point, then strain it into a jug. Rinse out the saucepan. Pour the milk into the egg mixture from a height, whisking constantly as you go – it helps to put a folded tea towel under your bowl to stop it moving around. When you have added all the milk, pour it back into the saucepan. Put the pan over a low heat and stir constantly for a few minutes until the mixture starts to thicken. Do not leave it unattended as the mixture will thicken on the bottom very quickly and may burn.

When the mixture has thickened enough to coat the back of a spoon, divide it between 6 shallow ramekins. Leave them to cool, then cover them loosely, place them on a tray and chill in the fridge for several hours, preferably overnight.

Just before you want to serve the puddings, sprinkle the top of each one with a tablespoon of sugar. Caramelise the sugar with a blowtorch – or put the puddings under a preheated grill for a few minutes. The sugar will darken and bubble up. Leave the puddings to cool so the crust sets and hardens before serving.

CLEMENTINE OR BLOOD ORANGE SORBET

SERVES 4-6

This is a very fresh and quite grown-up sorbet. We've included liquid glucose in this recipe, as it stops sugar crystals from forming so helps the sorbet keep better. You can find it in supermarkets but if you don't have any, use an extra 50g of sugar or 50g of mild runny honey. We like to glam up the sorbet with a drop of Campari – or Limoncello in the lemon version.

150g caster sugar
50ml liquid glucose
zest of 6 clementines or
3 blood oranges
250ml clementine or
blood orange juice
2 tbsp Campari (optional)

Put the caster sugar and liquid glucose into a saucepan with 200ml of water and the citrus zest. Heat slowly, stirring until the sugar has dissolved, then bring it to the boil and simmer for 2 minutes. Remove the pan from the heat and leave the sugar syrup to infuse with the zest until it has cooled to room temperature.

Add the citrus juice, then strain everything through a sieve. Stir in the Campari, if using, then chill the mixture in the fridge for at least a couple of hours. Alternatively, put it in the freezer for half an hour.

To make the sorbet, churn the mixture in an ice-cream maker until frozen, then scoop it into a freezer container. If you don't have an ice-cream maker, put the mixture in a shallow container and pop it into the freezer. Remove it from the freezer every half hour and whisk thoroughly, preferably with a hand-held whisk, to get as much air into it as possible. Do this at least 3 or 4 times until the mixture is frozen so hard it's not possible to whisk it any more. To serve, remove the sorbet from the freezer and leave it in the fridge for half an hour before you want to serve it.

Lemon with Limoncello
You can also make a lovely lemon version. Use the zest of 3 lemons and 200–250ml of lemon juice, depending on how sharp you want your sorbet. Add 2 tablespoons of Limoncello if you want to include alcohol.

NUTELLA ICE CREAM

SERVES 4-6

For fans of Nutella and ice cream what could be better than this?
To put it bluntly this gelato is 'proper badass', a dish of supreme
decadence. We like to add the shavings of dark chocolate to offset
the sweetness of the Nutella.

250ml milk
250ml double cream
100g caster sugar
1 vanilla pod, split
4 egg yolks
200g Nutella
100g dark chocolate
(optional)

Put the milk, cream, half the sugar and the vanilla pod in a saucepan. Heat gently and keep stirring until the sugar has dissolved. Remove the pan from the heat and leave the milk and cream to infuse.

Put the egg yolks and the remaining sugar in a bowl and whisk, preferably with a hand-held whisk, until the mixture turns a very pale yellow, is well-aerated and mousse-like in texture.

Strain the milk and cream mixture into a jug and discard the vanilla pod – you can scrape out the seeds if you like and add those to the mixture. Rinse out the saucepan and pour the contents back into it. Stir the mixture over a low heat until it is thick enough to coat the back of a spoon.

Remove the pan from the heat and leave it to cool down for a few minutes. Add the Nutella and stir until it has melted into the custard. Strain the custard into a container and leave it to cool to room temperature. Then chill it in the fridge for several hours, preferably overnight, before serving.

If using the chocolate, cut it into shards with a fairly sharp knife. Churn the custard in an ice-cream maker until thick, adding the chocolate towards the end of this process. Transfer the ice cream to a container and put it in the freezer.

If you don't have an ice-cream maker, pour the custard into a container and freeze immediately. Every half hour, take the mixture out and whisk it, then put it back in the freezer. Repeat this several times until the ice cream has completely set, adding the chocolate after the second time.

ORANGE AND ALMOND CAKE

SERVES 8–10

What could be more Mediterranean than oranges and almonds?
This is a real sunshine cake and will cheer you up on a grey day
in Blighty. And what's more it is flour free and fabulous.

2 small oranges
butter, for greasing
6 eggs
225g caster sugar
250g ground almonds
1 tsp baking powder
250ml crème fraiche or
whipped cream, to serve

To decorate
75g flaked almonds,
lightly toasted
2 tbsp icing sugar
2 tsp very finely grated
orange zest

Put the whole oranges in a saucepan and cover them with water. Bring them to the boil, cover the pan with a lid and simmer for up to 2 hours, or until you can pierce the skin of the orange with the handle of a wooden spoon. Drain the oranges and cool them under running water. Break them open, remove any pips and blitz the oranges in a food processor or blender until smooth. Set aside.

Preheat the oven to 180°C/Fan 160°C/Gas 4. Grease a 23cm cake tin, preferably one with a loose bottom, and line the base with baking paper.

Put the eggs in a large bowl and whisk until very well aerated and frothy – the texture should be almost mousse-like. Gradually add the sugar, whisking constantly as you do so. Mix the ground almonds and baking powder together, then fold them into the mixture. Finally add the orange purée.

Pour the mixture into the prepared cake tin. Bake in the oven for 50 minutes to an hour, until the cake has shrunk away from the sides slightly and is firm but springy to the touch. Leave the cake to cool in the tin for 15 minutes, then turn it out on to a cooling rack. It might dip in the middle slightly as it cools, but don't worry.

Mix the flaked almonds with the icing sugar and orange zest, making sure the orange zest is evenly distributed. Sprinkle this over the cake. Serve with dollops of crème fraiche or whipped cream.

CHOCOLATE CHESTNUT CAKE

SERVES 8–10

They do great charcuterie in Corsica and they love chestnuts too. The wife of the one of the charcuterie producers we met made us a chestnut cake that was amazing and it inspired our recipe. This is moist and fudgy – a cross between a regular sponge and a truffle cake and it's even better after a day or two. Do hunt out the chestnut flour if you can. Some supermarkets stock it.

200g butter, diced, plus extra for greasing

200g dark chocolate (70% cocoa solids)

6 eggs, separated

150g caster sugar

1 tsp vanilla extract

150g whole chestnuts (vacuum-packed are fine)

100g chestnut flour or ground almonds

Topping

2 tbsp icing sugar

250ml whipping cream

chocolate, grated or in curls, to decorate

Preheat the oven to 180°C/Fan 160°C/Gas 4. Grease a loose-bottomed 23cm cake tin with butter and line the base with baking paper. Put the butter and chocolate in a heatproof bowl and place it over a pan of very gently simmering water – make sure the bottom of the bowl doesn't touch the water. Stir regularly until the butter and chocolate are melted and well combined. Allow to cool slightly.

Whisk the egg yolks and sugar together until very pale yellow and well aerated. Gradually pour the chocolate and butter into the egg yolk and sugar mixture, gently stirring to combine, then add the vanilla extract. Crumble the chestnuts and fold them into the chocolate mixture. Sieve the chestnut flour and fold this in too. If using the ground almonds, just break up any clumps and fold them in.

Whisk the egg whites until they're stiff and dry. Using a metal spoon, add about a quarter of the egg whites to the chocolate mixture – it will seem very stiff to start with. Make sure the egg whites are completely dispersed through the chocolate before adding more. Continue to fold the rest of the egg whites into the mixture – do this in about 4 batches in total. Pour the mixture into the tin and bake for 30–35 minutes until springy on top. Test with a cake skewer – it won't come out completely clean and will probably have moist crumbs attached.

Leave the cake to cool in the tin, then turn it out. Don't worry if the surface cracks – it all adds to the rustic charm. When you're ready to serve, whisk the icing sugar into the cream and whip until it forms soft peaks that hold their shape. Pile the cream on top of the cake and top with grated chocolate or chocolate curls.

OLIVE OIL LOAF CAKE

SERVES 8–10

Olive oil is not just for salads – it's great in baking too. This is one of those dead simple cakes that you can't get enough of. Because of the oil, the texture is moister than a sponge in a cloudburst.

3 eggs
150g caster sugar
zest and juice of 1 lemon
150ml olive oil
100ml milk
200g plain flour
1 tbsp baking powder

Preheat the oven to 200°C/Fan 180°C/Gas 6. Line a large loaf tin with baking paper or spray it with cake-release spray.

Using a stand mixer or an electric beater, whisk the eggs, sugar and lemon zest together until well aerated – the texture should be soft and mousse-like. Continue to whisk while drizzling in the olive oil, little by little, followed by the lemon juice and the milk.

Sift the flour and baking powder into a bowl, making sure they are well combined. Add them to the cake batter in 3 batches, folding each batch in thoroughly but gently. The batter will be very runny but don't worry.

Pour the cake batter into the prepared loaf tin. Bake it for 45–50 minutes until a skewer comes out clean. Cool the cake in the tin for 10 minutes, then turn it out on to a rack and leave to cool completely.

TIRAMISU

SERVES 6-8

Everyone loves this Italian favourite… especially Mrs Myers. Ours is a classic recipe and we think it's just right. It freezes very well too so is a great pud to make if you want to get ahead with cooking for a special night. To defrost, just remove the tiramisu from the freezer a few hours before you want to serve it and leave it in the fridge.

2 eggs, separated, plus 2 egg yolks

50g caster sugar

250g mascarpone

200g double cream

50ml sweet Marsala

25ml golden rum or brandy

200ml strong espresso

16 boudoir or savoiardi biscuits

cocoa powder, for dusting

Put the egg yolks in a large bowl. Add the caster sugar and the mascarpone and whisk until the mixture is a pale yellow and completely lump free. Whisk the egg whites until they have reached the soft peak stage – they will still be slightly wet and won't cling to the bowl in the way stiffly whipped egg whites will. Whisk the double cream until it is aerated, thickened and forms loose, soft peaks.

Fold the egg whites and double cream into the mascarpone mixture as gently as you can. The mixture will look slightly grainy to start with, but keep folding until it is smooth, trying to make sure you leave as much air in as possible.

Put the Marsala, rum or brandy and the coffee into a shallow bowl. Dip the biscuits into the liquid, one at a time. Arrange half of them in the base of 8 serving dishes or glasses or in one large trifle bowl. Dust over a little cocoa powder, then top with half the mascarpone mix. Dip the rest of the biscuits into the Marsala mixture and arrange them lightly over the first layers, then top with the rest of the mascarpone. Dust again with plenty more cocoa.

Cover the dishes or bowl with cling film and chill for several hours, preferably overnight. Serve well chilled.

TARTE TROPÉZIENNE

SERVES 8–10

This isn't really a tart – more of a rich brioche-style cake stuffed with creamy filling – but it does hail from St Trop. It is said to have been invented for the young Brigitte Bardot who was filming there at the time. And what's good enough for BB is good enough for us. BTW, you'll find pearl sugar nibs in the cake decorating section at the supermarket. We have to admit that this one is easiest to do in a stand mixer, as it involves a lot of kneading.

Brioche

300g strong white bread flour

7g dried yeast

50g caster sugar

pinch of salt

2 eggs

75ml tepid milk

½ tsp vanilla extract

a few drops of orange blossom water or almond extract

100g butter, softened

oil, for greasing

Crème patissière

1 vanilla pod, split lengthways

300ml whole milk

4 egg yolks

75g caster sugar

50g cornflour

200ml whipping cream

To make the brioche, put the flour, yeast and sugar into the bowl of a stand mixer. Stir, then add a good pinch of salt. Beat the eggs well in a separate bowl, then stir in the milk and add the vanilla extract and the orange blossom water or almond extract. With the motor running on its slowest setting, gradually incorporate the wet ingredients into the dry. Keep kneading on a low speed until you have a smooth dough, then start incorporating the butter. Add a spoonful at a time, making sure it is fully mixed with the dough before adding any more. Once you have added it all, keep kneading the dough for at least another 5 minutes until it is shiny and elastic.

Cover the dough with oiled cling film or a damp tea towel and leave it somewhere warm to prove for a couple of hours or until it has doubled in volume. Knock it back and shape it into a tight ball, then leave it to chill in the fridge for a couple of hours – or overnight if you prefer. This will stop the dough proving too quickly.

To make the crème patissière, put the vanilla pod and milk in a pan and heat gently. Beat the egg yolks and sugar in a bowl until pale and mousse-like, then beat in the cornflour. Gradually add the heated milk, pouring it in from a height and whisking constantly, then rinse out your pan. Pour the mixture into the pan and very slowly bring it to the boil, stirring constantly – be careful as the mixture can suddenly thicken on the base of the pan. When the mixture is the texture of thick custard, remove the pan from the heat and discard the vanilla pod. Push the mixture through a sieve to get rid of any lumps. Cover with cling film, making sure the film is touching the crème pat – this will prevent a skin from forming. Allow it to cool, then chill thoroughly in the fridge for at least 2 hours. Whisk the cream to the soft peak stage. Stir a tablespoon into the crème patissière to loosen it, then fold in the rest.

Topping

beaten egg, for
brushing
50g pearl sugar nibs

Line a baking sheet with baking paper. Pat the dough into a circle with a diameter of 23–25cm. Cover it again and leave it to rise for at least another hour until puffed up. Preheat the oven to 200°C/Fan 180°C/Gas 6. Brush the dough with beaten egg and sprinkle with the sugar nibs, making sure the whole surface is covered. Bake in the oven for 20–25 minutes until the dough is well risen and golden brown. If the cake starts to get too brown, cover it with foil. Remove it from the oven and place it on a rack to cool down.

To assemble, cut the cake in half horizontally, being careful not to upturn the top and spill all the pearl sugar. Set the top aside. Pipe the crème patissière over the bottom half of the cake or spread it evenly with a spatula. Replace the top. Chill the cake for at least an hour, then slice and serve.

TORTA MENJAR BLANC

CUSTARD TART

SERVES 8-10

Dare we say it but at first glance this looked a bit boring. Oh, how wrong can you be? It's a double-crust tart filled with rich custard and has a beautiful, delicate flavour. We cooked it in Spain and it was so good – not one for diet days though!

1 litre whole milk
1 vanilla pod, split lengthways
pared zest from 1 lemon
6 egg yolks
150g caster sugar
100g cornflour
egg white, to wash
icing sugar, to serve (optional)

Pastry
350g plain flour
150g icing sugar
pinch of salt
175g butter, chilled and diced
grated zest of 1 lemon
2 eggs, beaten

First make the pastry. Mix the flour and icing sugar with a pinch of salt, then rub in the butter. Stir in the lemon zest and then add the eggs, a little at a time, until you have a smooth dough. Shape the dough into 2 balls, one slightly larger than the other, and wrap them in cling film. Chill them for at least an hour, but preferably overnight.

To make the filling, pour the milk into a saucepan and add the vanilla pod and zest. Bring the milk to the boil, then remove the pan from the heat and leave the milk to infuse until it has cooled to room temperature. Whisk the egg yolks and caster sugar together until they've increased in volume and have a moussy texture. Sieve the cornflour and whisk this into the egg and sugar mixture until well combined.

Reheat the milk and strain it into a jug. Rinse the saucepan. Pour the milk from a height in a steady stream over the egg and sugar mixture, whisking constantly, then pour everything back into the saucepan. Stir constantly over a medium heat until the custard has thickened – this will take about 5 minutes. Transfer the custard to a jug or bowl and cover with cling film, making sure it touches the custard to prevent it from forming a skin. Chill until you are ready to bake the tart.

Roll out the larger piece of pastry and use it to line a 23cm tart or a shallow cake tin – preferably a loose-bottomed one. Trim. Pierce the pastry all over with a fork and chill it for half an hour. Preheat the oven to 180°C/Fan 160°C/Gas 4. Spread the chilled custard over the base of the tart. Roll out the remaining piece of dough on a piece of baking paper, chill it for 10 minutes, then use it to cover the tart. Dampen the edges with water and crimp together. Brush the tart with egg white and bake it in the oven for 40 minutes. Remove from the oven, then allow it to cool before chilling. Serve dusted with icing sugar if you like.

BREAD AND BUTTER PUDDING

WITH PEDRO XIMÉNEZ SHERRY

SERVES 6

Most countries have their version of bread and butter pudding because no one wants to waste leftover bread. This is the old favourite with a Spanish kick, laced with some fantastic Pedro Ximénez sherry and a whiff of cinnamon and orange. It's good enough to get the vicar round for tea.

100g raisins
100ml Pedro Ximénez or very sweet sherry
butter, for spreading and greasing
6 slices of brioche or plain panettone
zest of 1 orange
1 tsp cinnamon
4 eggs
50g soft light brown sugar
350ml whole milk
150ml double cream
1 tbsp demerara sugar

Put the raisins in a small saucepan and cover them with the sherry. Heat gently until the sherry is almost at boiling point, then remove the pan from the heat and leave the raisins to cool. They should absorb most of the sherry and plump up nicely. Strain the raisins, making sure you reserve any juices.

Generously butter a 1.5 litre oven dish. Butter the slices of brioche or panettone and cut each slice into 4 triangles. Arrange a layer of the bread, butter-side up, in the oven dish. Sprinkle two-thirds of the raisins over the bread, then add most of the orange zest and cinnamon – you'll find it's easiest to grate the zest directly over the pudding. Arrange the remaining bread slices over the top, butter-side up again.

Gently beat the eggs with the sugar – you don't want them aerated, just well combined. Gradually stir in the milk and double cream, then add any reserved juices from the raisins. Strain the mixture into a jug, then pour it over the bread and raisins. Do this very slowly, giving the egg mixture time to soak into the bread so it doesn't dislodge and float out of place.

Sprinkle over the remaining raisins. Combine the rest of the zest and cinnamon with the demerara sugar and sprinkle this over the pudding. Leave the pudding to stand for about 20 minutes to allow the custard to soak into the bread. Preheat the oven to 180°C/Fan 160°C/Gas 4. Bake the pudding for 35–40 minutes, until the top layer of bread is crisp and a rich caramelised brown in places.

ZABAGLIONE

WITH ORANGE AND ALMOND BISCUITS

SERVES 4–6

Lush and creamy, zabaglione is one of the great Italian puds. It's amazing as is but it's well worth making these crunchy little almond biscuits to go with it. And if any biscuits are left over, enjoy them with your coffee the next day.

6 egg yolks
100g sugar
75ml sweet Marsala wine or Vin Santo
1 piece of pared orange zest

Orange and almond biscuits
150g ground almonds
150g plain flour
100g softened butter
100g caster sugar
zest of 1 orange
1 egg, beaten
a few drops of almond extract (optional)

For the zabaglione, put the egg yolks, sugar, Marsala or Vin Santo and the orange zest into a heatproof bowl. Set the bowl over a saucepan of simmering water, making sure that the bottom of the bowl does not touch the water.

Whisk the contents of the bowl until very light and fluffy. Use an electric hand-held whisk if possible and it will take anything from 5–10 minutes. You will know the mixture is ready when you can form a ribbon along the surface with your beaters. Divide the mixture between 6 small or 4 medium dishes or glasses. You can serve this right away or leave it to cool down. Serve the zabaglione with the orange and almond biscuits on the side.

For the orange and almond biscuits, mix the ground almonds with the flour in a bowl. Cream the butter and sugar with a hand-held whisk in a separate bowl or in a stand mixer until soft, fluffy and white. Add the orange zest and egg with 2 tablespoons of the almond and flour mixture and stir to combine. Add the almond extract, if using, then the rest of the ground almonds and flour, working the mixture as little as possible. You will end up with quite a soft dough.

Divide the dough into 2 pieces and shape them into 2 logs about 5–6cm in diameter. Wrap them in cling film and chill for at least 2 hours until very firm. When you are ready to bake the biscuits, preheat the oven to 180°C/Fan 160°C/Gas 4. Cut each log into 12 slices and place them, evenly spaced, on 2 baking trays. Bake the biscuits for 10–12 minutes until they are a light golden brown, then place them on a rack to cool.

RICE PUDDING
WITH APRICOT COMPOTE
SERVES 6

They love their rice pud in Spain where it is called arroz con leche. This is the best we've ever tasted, with some lovely Moorish spicing. We also like to add a fruit compote, such as this one with apricots. The fruit should keep its shape and not turn to mush – it's nice on its own too.

1 litre whole milk

1 cinnamon stick

1 piece of pared lemon zest

1 piece of pared orange zest

125g pudding rice

100g caster sugar

250ml single cream

2 egg yolks

Apricot compote

50g caster sugar or honey

1 vanilla pod, split

12 small apricots

To make the rice pudding, put the milk into a saucepan with the cinnamon stick and the lemon and orange zests. Bring the milk to the boil, then turn down the heat and sprinkle in the rice and sugar. Stir over a medium heat until the sugar has dissolved, then continue to cook, stirring constantly, for another 5 minutes. Reduce the heat so the rice is simmering very gently, then leave it to cook for a further 35–40 minutes, stirring regularly. If it looks as though it is becoming too thick, add a little more milk.

Remove the pan from the heat and leave to cool a little. Beat the cream and egg yolks together, then stir them into the rice. Discard the cinnamon stick and zest. You can serve this while it is warm and fairly runny or leave it to chill and thicken up. If chilling the pudding, make sure that cling film is touching the rice so a skin doesn't form. Serve the rice pudding with spoonfuls of compote.

For the apricot compote, put the sugar or honey into a saucepan with the vanilla pod. Pour in 175ml of water, then stir over a low heat until the sugar has dissolved. Turn up the heat and simmer for 5 minutes until the mixture looks syrupy, then add the apricots. Turn the heat down again and simmer until the apricots are just tender, but nowhere near collapsing – this should take 10–15 minutes.

ROASTED FIGS

WITH HONEY

SERVES 4

There's nothing like a sun-warmed fig, picked straight from the tree, but figs are also great cooked. This is a doddle to make and a really lovely pud.

15g butter, plus extra
for greasing
8 figs (or 12 if
particularly small)
25g honey
juice of ½ orange
½ tsp cinnamon

To serve
150ml mascarpone
1 tsp honey
50ml double cream
1 tsp orange
blossom water
1 tsp orange zest
1 tbsp flaked almonds,
lightly toasted (optional)

Preheat the oven to 200°C/Fan 180°C/Gas 6. Butter a baking dish large enough to hold the figs snugly.

Trim the top of the fig stalks. Cut a deep cross in each of the figs, almost to the base, but make sure each quarter is still attached. Squeeze the sides of the figs gently to expose more of their flesh. Arrange them in the baking dish.

Melt the butter and honey in a small saucepan and whisk in the orange juice and cinnamon. Drizzle this over the figs, then roast them in the preheated oven for 15 minutes.

To serve, whisk the mascarpone and honey together. Whisk the double cream until it's soft and billowy (it should still drop off a spoon), then fold it into the mascarpone with the orange blossom water and orange zest.

Serve the figs with the cream mixture and sprinkle over the flaked almonds, if using.

'DRUNK' PEACHES

SERVES 4

This is based on the Elizabeth David classic, which involves dropping peach slices into a glass of dessert wine. Thanks, Elizabeth, this is so simple and if you get really good peaches – the white sort are great – and good nutty-flavoured dessert wine, it's a wonderful dessert. Mrs Myers approves.

4 peaches
200–300ml dessert wine
50g flaked almonds
(optional)

Cut the peaches into wedges, about 8 per peach, peeling off the skin as you go. Drop the slices into wine glasses or small sundae dishes. Pour the dessert wine over them – the amount you will need depends on the size of your glass and how well packed the peaches are, but 50–75ml per glass should be about right. Do not quite cover the peaches – they should be just poking through the wine. Leave them to stand for a couple of minutes before serving.

If using the flaked almonds, toast them very lightly in a dry frying pan until they're lightly coloured. Sprinkle them over the peaches.

And if you're feeling really luxurious you could add some Chantilly cream – whipped double cream with a tablespoon of icing sugar folded through it.

APRICOT AND ALMOND TART

SERVES 8–10

A tart with a Moorish heart – the almonds and orange blossom water go so well with the apricots. Put it all in a melt-in-the mouth pastry case and you have a sweet taste of the Med. If you're not keen on orange blossom water, leave it out and just use some almond extract in the frangipane instead.

Pastry

225g plain flour

50g caster sugar

125g butter

pinch of salt

1 egg yolk

2 tbsp cold milk

Apricots

50ml honey

2 tsp orange blossom water (optional)

1 tbsp rum

8 ripe, but firm apricots, halved and stoned

Frangipane

85g butter, softened

85g caster sugar

3 eggs

85g ground almonds

1 tsp orange blossom water or a few drops of almond extract

To serve

crème fraiche

First make the pastry. Put the flour, sugar and butter in a bowl and add a pinch of salt. Rub the butter into the dry ingredients, until the texture resembles fine breadcrumbs. Add the egg yolk and drizzle in the cold milk, working the mixture as little as possible until you have a smooth dough. You can do this in a stand mixer or food processor if you prefer. Form the dough into a ball, wrap it in cling film and chill for at least half an hour.

Preheat the oven to 200°C/Fan 180°/Gas 6. Lightly flour a work surface and roll out the pastry and use it to line a 28cm diameter tart dish. Cover the pastry with baking paper and fill it with baking beans. Bake the pastry case in the oven for 15 minutes, then remove the baking paper and beans and cook it for a further 5 minutes. Remove the pastry case from the oven and leave it to cool.

For the apricots, heat the honey, orange blossom water, if using, and rum in a small saucepan. Put the apricots in a roasting tin, skin-side down, and pour the honey mixture over them. Roast the apricots for 15 minutes, then flip them over and roast them for a further 5–10 minutes. The apricots should keep their shape but feel tender when pierced with a knife tip. You can cook them at the same time as the pastry case. Remove the apricots from the oven and leave them to cool.

To make the frangipane, cream the butter and sugar until fluffy. Fold in the eggs one at a time, adding a third of the ground almonds each time. Add the orange blossom water or almond extract. Spread the frangipane over the base of the pastry case, then arrange the apricots on top, reserving any syrupy liquid from the roasting tin. Bake the tart for about 30 minutes, until the filling is just set and a light golden brown. Remove it from the oven and brush it with the reserved syrup, then put it back in the oven for another 5 minutes. Serve hot or cold with crème fraiche.

ORANGE FLAN

SERVES 6

A Kingy favourite this – basically an orange-flavoured crème caramel, known as 'flan' in Spain. You'll have lots of egg whites left from this so how about making the cherry meringues on page 302?

500ml orange juice
zest of 1 orange
150g caster sugar
8 egg yolks
2 eggs

Caramel
75g caster sugar

To make the caramel, put the sugar in a medium saucepan and shake so it spreads into an even layer. Pour over 25ml of water – it will just moisten the sugar enough to give it the consistency of wet sand. Set the pan over a medium heat and leave the sugar to melt. Do not stir or touch it, but give the pan a swirl every so often. The sugar will melt and eventually turn a rich golden brown. Watch it very closely and if it looks like one edge is darkening much quicker than the rest, shift the saucepan around so it is moved away from the heat slightly.

When the colour is just slightly lighter than a caramel should be, remove the pan from the heat – the sugar will continue to cook as it cools. Working very quickly, pour the caramel into a medium-sized oven dish. If the caramel starts to set before you have finished, reheat it very gently and continue. Leave to cool.

Pour the orange juice into a saucepan and add the orange zest and sugar. Heat gently, stirring until the sugar has dissolved, then bring it to the boil for 2 minutes. Remove the pan from the heat and transfer the mixture to a jug. Preheat the oven to 150°C/Fan 130°C/Gas 2.

Put the eggs yolks in a large bowl, then crack in the whole eggs and break them all up with a fork until smooth. Do not use a whisk as you need to avoid beating air bubbles into the eggs. Gradually pour the orange juice mixture into the eggs from a height, stirring constantly and gently as you go. Strain the mixture, then pour it into the oven dish. Put the oven dish into a roasting tin. Pour boiling water into the tin until it comes up halfway to two-thirds up the sides of the oven dish. Cover with foil. Carefully place the tin in the oven and cook for 50–60 minutes. The flan will be done when it is firm around the outsides with a slight wobble in the middle.

Remove the flan from the oven and leave it to cool, then cover with cling film and chill in the fridge for several hours, or overnight, before serving.

CHERRY JAM

MAKES ABOUT 3 SMALL JARS

We went to visit some fruit growers near the town of Céret in southwest France and Christine made us this lovely jam – and the apricot jam opposite. She explained to us that the amount of sugar depends on the type of cherry you use. With sour or Morello cherries (which do have the best flavour for jam), use equal measures of cherries and sugar. If using sweet cherries, use slightly less – about 400g.

500g cherries
(pitted weight)
400–500g sugar
(depending on whether
you are using sweet or
sour cherries)
juice of 1 lemon

To sterilise your jam jars, run them through the hottest setting of your dishwasher, or wash them in plenty of hot, soapy water and leave them to dry in a low oven. Put a couple of saucers in the freezer to chill.

Pit the cherries and cut them in half, or quarters if they are particularly large. Do this over a bowl to catch any juice that might otherwise escape.

Put the cherries in a large saucepan or a preserving pan with any juice and a couple of tablespoons of water. Simmer very gently for a few minutes to soften the cherries, then add the sugar and lemon juice. Continue to simmer gently, stirring until the sugar has completely dissolved, then turn up the heat.

Bring the jam to a rolling boil until the setting point is reached. Start testing for this after 5 minutes. Use a thermometer – it should reach 105°C – or do the wrinkle test by dropping a little jam on to one of the chilled saucers and allowing it to cool. If the jam wrinkles when you push it with your finger, it has reached the setting point.

Allow the jam to cool a little, then stir it vigorously to get rid of any froth that might collect on top. Spoon the jam into the jars (a jar funnel is helpful, but not essential). Leave the jam to cool, then store it in a cool, dark place. Keep the jam in the fridge once opened.

APRICOT JAM

MAKES ABOUT 3 SMALL JARS

We picked some apricots with the fruit growers too and Christine gave us some of her delicious apricot jam to taste. Apparently it's traditional to add the apricot kernels and it gives the jam a hint of almond flavour.

500g apricots
(stoned weight)
500g sugar
juice of 1 lemon

To sterilise your jam jars, run them through the hottest setting of your dishwasher, or wash them in plenty of hot, soapy water and leave them to dry in a low oven. Put a couple of saucers in the freezer to chill.

Stone the apricots and dice them roughly. Crack some of the kernels lightly and tie them into a piece of muslin, then set them aside. Reserve a few more to add to the jam jars.

Put the apricots into a large saucepan or a preserving pan with 100ml of water. Simmer very gently for a few minutes until the apricots have softened and started to break down, then add the sugar and lemon juice. Continue to simmer gently, while stirring, until the sugar has completely dissolved.

Turn up the heat and bring the jam to a rolling boil until the setting point is reached, stirring regularly to make sure it doesn't catch. Start testing after about 10 minutes. Use a thermometer – it should reach 105°C – or do the wrinkle test by dropping a little jam on to one of the chilled saucers and allowing it to cool. If the jam wrinkles when you push it with your finger, it has reached setting point.

Allow the jam to cool a little, then stir it vigorously to get rid of any froth that might have collected on top. Discard the bag of kernels. Spoon the jam into the jars (a jar funnel is helpful, but not essential). Leave the jam to cool, then store in a cool, dark place. Keep it in the fridge once opened.

CHERRY MERINGUES

MAKES 12

Mediterranean food is seasonal and people like to celebrate the arrival of ingredients. Well, nothing has more festivals and parties in its honour than the cherry and this is our contribution. It's a proper party for cherries and a recipe we know you will want to make.

400g caster sugar
8 egg whites
4 tbsp cherry compote
(see below)

Cherry compote
600g ripe, pitted cherries
50g caster sugar
1 vanilla pod, split
1 tbsp Kirsch (optional)
a few drops of almond
extract (optional)

To serve
400g double cream,
whipped

For the compote, put the cherries in a saucepan and sprinkle over the sugar. Add the vanilla pod. Heat gently until the sugar has melted, stirring regularly and squashing down the cherries to help release their liquid. When the sugar has melted, cover the pan and simmer over a very low heat for 15–20 minutes, checking and stirring regularly to make sure nothing is catching. When the cherries are soft, remove the pan from the heat and stir in the Kirsch and the almond extract, if using. Leave it to cool.

To make the meringues, preheat the oven to 200°C/Fan 180°C/Gas 6. Put the caster sugar in an ovenproof dish and place it in the oven for 4–5 minutes. The aim is to just heat the sugar without it melting and this will help stop the meringues from weeping later. Reduce the oven temperature to 110°C/Fan 90°C/Gas¼, and line 2 baking trays with non-stick baking paper.

Whisk the egg whites with an electric hand-held whisk until they reach the soft peak stage, then gradually pour in the caster sugar, with the whisk still running, until it is all incorporated. Keep whisking until the meringue has cooled down.

Take 4 tablespoons of the compote and whizz very briefly in a food processor – make sure it isn't smooth, you want chunks of cherries. Using large spoons, dollop 12 large mounds of meringue on to the baking trays, adding some of the whizzed compote to each one. Make sure the meringues have some space between them. Put them in the preheated oven and bake for 2 hours, until they are dry and firm, with a little softness in the middle. Turn off the oven and leave the meringues until completely cool. Serve them with the whipped cream and cherry compote.

WATERMELON AND ROSE JELLY

SERVES 6

They love refreshing jellies like these in southern Italy and they often garnish them with jasmine flowers – or you could use fresh, dried or crystallised rose petals. Who says the Bikers can't do dainty! The amount of watermelon needed to make the juice for this will vary slightly, depending on how heavily seeded it is, so we've given a range. And the amount of sugar depends on how sweet your melon is, so taste and add enough to get the flavour you like.

750–850g watermelon flesh
7 gelatine leaves
50–75g caster sugar
1 tbsp lemon juice
1 tbsp rose water

Garnish
a few jasmine or rose petals
2 tbsp pistachio nibs (skinless)

First make the watermelon juice. Blitz the watermelon flesh in a blender, then push it through a very fine sieve. You need 600ml of juice, but if it falls slightly short you can make up the difference with water or any other juice you may have. Leave the juice for a while to allow any foam or bubbles to disperse.

Put the gelatine leaves in a bowl and cover them with cold water. Leave them to soften for 2–3 minutes.

Taste the juice. If your watermelon is very ripe and sweet, use 50g of sugar, but if you think it needs more help, use 75g. Put the juice in a saucepan with the sugar and lemon juice. Stir the mixture over a very low heat until the sugar is dissolved, then bring it almost to boiling point. Wring out the gelatine and add it to the pan. Stir until the gelatine has melted, making sure you do not allow the mixture to boil, then remove the pan from the heat and add the rose water.

Strain the mixture through a sieve into a jug, then pour it into a mould or into individual glasses. Try to pour as slowly and steadily as you can – you do not want to create air bubbles in your jelly.

Let the jelly cool, then cover and leave in the fridge to chill and set. Garnish with jasmine or rose petals and a few pistachio nibs.

BASICS

POLENTA

SERVES 4

We like eating this with the Calabrian pork ribs on page 54 but it's great for soaking up the juices of a good stew too.

750ml just-boiled water
250ml whole milk
pinch of salt
200g coarse cornmeal
75g butter, diced
50g Parmesan cheese, grated

Pour the water and milk into a large saucepan and bring them to the boil. Add a good pinch of salt, then sprinkle in the cornmeal, whisking constantly as you do so.

Turn down the heat and cook the polenta, uncovered, for 45–60 minutes, stirring very regularly to make sure it doesn't catch on the bottom. It's done when it starts coming away from the sides and you can trace a clear path with your spoon along the bottom of the pan.

Beat in the butter and cheese until thoroughly combined and serve immediately.

FRESH PASTA

MAKES ABOUT 600G

Making pasta is fun and not nearly as hard as you think once you get the hang of it. Use this recipe to make pasta for the lasagne on pages 52–53.

500g Italian '00' flour
5 eggs
pinch of salt

If making your pasta by hand, sift the flour into a bowl, then turn it out on to a clean work surface. Make a large well in the middle, break the eggs into it and add a generous pinch of salt.

Break up all the yolks, then using a circular motion with your fingers, start working in the flour from the sides. When you have worked most of it in, start shaping the dough into a ball. If it is still on the dry side, wet your hands – this should give enough extra liquid to work the dough together. When the dough has formed a ball, knead it for about 10 minutes until smooth. It will still feel quite firm at this stage.

If you're making the pasta in a stand mixer, sift the flour and salt into the bowl and fit the dough hook. With the motor running on a slow setting, gradually add the eggs, one at a time, until the mixture comes together. Knead the dough in the mixer for about 5 minutes.

Divide the dough into 2 balls, wrap them in cling film and leave them to rest for an hour before rolling. You can freeze the dough at this stage if you like.

To roll the pasta, flatten each piece of dough down slightly and start on the widest setting of your pasta machine. Roll the pasta through, then move down a setting. Repeat twice more, reducing the setting each time, then fold the pasta in half and start again. Repeat the procedure. By this point the pasta will be very long so cut it in half. Put one of the pieces under a damp cloth, then fold the other piece into 3 – it should be the same width as the machine if you give it one turn. Roll through again, starting at the widest setting then reducing until it is about 1.5mm thick. Cut the pasta as required – for lasagne sheets, cut it to fit your lasagne dish. Otherwise cut it into thick ribbons (pappardelle) about 2cm wide, or into thinner tagliatelle.

You can use this pasta fresh or dry. To dry the lengths, lay them out over a pasta drier (a clothes horse also works well), or roll the ribbons into loose nests. Leave them to dry out completely, then store in a cool dark place until needed.

TOMATO SAUCE

MAKES ABOUT 1 LITRE

We've included various versions of tomato sauce in this book but this is the basic recipe and ideal to use in the lasagne on pages 52–53.

6 tbsp olive oil

2 onions, very finely sliced

6 garlic cloves, finely chopped

250ml red wine

4 x 400g cans of tomatoes or 1.5kg plum tomatoes, peeled and chopped

2 tsp dried oregano

1 tsp fresh thyme leaves

2 bay leaves

pinch of sugar (optional)

salt and black pepper

Heat the olive oil in a large saucepan and add the onions. Sauté them very gently until very soft – this will take at least 15 minutes.

Add the garlic and cook for another 3–4 minutes over a very gentle heat, then pour in the red wine. Boil until the wine is reduced by at least half, then add the tomatoes and herbs. Season with salt and pepper.

Bring the sauce to the boil, then turn down the heat, cover the pan and simmer for an hour. At this point taste the sauce and if it seems acidic, add a generous pinch of sugar. Continue to simmer, uncovered, for about half an hour until well reduced.

HERB OIL

MAKES 1 BOTTLE

This beautifully fragrant oil is wonderful added to the bean casserole on page 108 and it's a great thing to have in your kitchen for adding to salads or slathering on a bit of toast.

75ml olive oil
1 garlic clove
zest of ½ lemon
small bunch of parsley leaves, finely chopped
small bunch of basil leaves, finely chopped
2 sprigs of tarragon, leaves finely chopped
1 sprig of rosemary, leaves finely chopped
1 tsp red wine vinegar
salt and black pepper

Put all the ingredients in a food processor and pulse until the herbs have broken down and combined well with the oil. The colour should be an intense dark green. Season with salt and pepper.

MAYONNAISE

MAKES A GOOD BOWLFUL

We love our mayo and this is dead simple to make. It's great with anything from chips to croquetas.

2 egg yolks
1 tsp mustard
250ml sunflower or groundnut oil
squeeze of lemon juice or a few drops of vinegar
salt and black pepper

Put the egg yolks in a bowl with the mustard and a little salt. Mix them together until well combined.

Start drizzling in the oil, a few drops at a time, whisking constantly, until the mixture has thickened. Keep adding the oil, very gradually, until you have incorporated it all. If it the mayonnaise seems to be becoming greasy or too thick to work with, add a few drops of warm water and whisk thoroughly before adding any more oil.

Taste the mayonnaise, then add more seasoning and a squeeze of lemon or a few drops of vinegar if you think it needs acidity.

VEGETABLE STOCK

MAKES ABOUT 1.5 LITRES

We developed this stock for our 'Go Veggie' book and it's a good 'un so we're including it here for use in soups and stews.

1 tbsp olive oil
2 large onions, roughly chopped
3 large carrots, well washed, chopped
200g squash or pumpkin, unpeeled, diced
4 celery sticks, sliced
2 leeks, sliced
100ml white wine or vermouth
1 large sprig of thyme
1 large sprig of parsley
1 bay leaf
a few peppercorns

Heat the olive oil in a large saucepan. Add all the vegetables and fry them over a high heat, stirring regularly, until they're starting to brown and caramelise around the edges. This will take at least 10 minutes. Add the white wine or vermouth and boil until it has evaporated away.

Cover the veg with 2 litres of water and add the herbs and peppercorns. Bring to the boil, then turn the heat down to a gentle simmer. Cook the stock, uncovered, for about an hour, stirring every so often.

Check the stock – the colour should have some depth to it. Strain it through a colander or a sieve lined with kitchen paper or muslin into a bowl and store it in the fridge for up to a week. Alternatively, pour the stock into freezer-proof containers and freeze.

CHICKEN STOCK

MAKES ABOUT 1 LITRE

You can buy good fresh chicken stock in supermarkets, but it's good to make your own sometimes. This recipe uses raw chicken and has loads of flavour.

several raw chicken backs or carcasses and 4 wings or 1kg chicken wings
1 large onion, unpeeled and quartered
1 large carrot, roughly chopped
2 celery sticks
2 bay leaves
a few black peppercorns
a sprig of thyme
a sprig of parsley
a few garlic cloves

Put the chicken into a large saucepan or stockpot. Cover it with plenty of cold water – the water should come to about 3cm above the chicken. Bring the water to the boil, then keep skimming off the mushroom-coloured foam that appears until it turns white.

Add all the remaining ingredients, partially cover the pan and simmer the stock gently for about 3 hours until it is a rich golden brown.

Strain the stock through a sieve lined with kitchen paper or muslin, but don't push the bits through if you want a clear stock. Discard all the solids. Leave the stock to cool to room temperature, then chill it in the fridge. When it is cold, you can remove any fat that's sitting on top.

You can store the stock in the fridge for up to 4 days, or freeze it. You can also reduce it down further to get a more concentrated flavour and freeze it in ice cube trays. Once frozen, turn the cubes out into a large bag or plastic container.

FISH STOCK

MAKES ABOUT 1.5 LITRES

You can buy fish stock but it does vary enormously in quality and it is really worth making this for the fish soup on page 166.

2kg fish heads and bones from white fish (ask your fishmonger)

1 tbsp salt

2 tbsp olive oil

1 onion, finely chopped

2 leeks, finely sliced

½ fennel bulb, finely chopped

1 celery stick, sliced

2 garlic cloves, sliced

200ml white wine

bouquet garni (2 sprigs each of parsley, tarragon and thyme)

2 bay leaves

a few peppercorns

1 piece of thinly pared lemon zest

Put the fish heads and bones in a bowl, cover them with cold water and add the salt. Leave them to stand for an hour, then drain and wash thoroughly under running water. This process helps to draw out any blood from the fish and gives you a much clearer, fresher-tasting stock.

Heat the olive oil in a large saucepan. Add the onion, leeks, fennel, celery and garlic. Cook the vegetables over a medium heat for several minutes until they have started to soften without taking on any colour.

Add the fish heads and bones and pour over the wine. Bring to the boil, then add 2 litres of water. Bring back to the boil, skim off any mushroom-coloured foam that appears, then turn the heat down to a very slow simmer. Add the herbs, peppercorns and lemon zest and leave to simmer for half an hour, skimming off any foam every so often.

Strain the stock through a colander or sieve, then line the sieve with kitchen paper or muslin and strain the stock again – do not push it through as that will result in a cloudier stock. Transfer the stock to a container and chill it in the fridge. It will keep for 3–4 days in the fridge, or can be frozen for 3 months.

COOKING CHICKPEAS

Canned chickpeas are fine but for some dishes, such as the pasta with chickpeas on page 43, fresh really are best. It's worth cooking up a load of chickpeas and stashing them in the freezer. If you want to do a smaller amount, 100 grams of dried chickpeas makes about 220 grams of cooked.

500g dried chickpeas

4 garlic cloves, lightly crushed in their skins

2 sprigs of thyme or rosemary

2 sprigs of parsley

1 tsp salt

2.5 litres vegetable or chicken stock or water

Put the chickpeas in a large bowl, cover them with cold water and leave them to soak overnight.

The next day, drain and rinse them and put them in a saucepan with the garlic, herbs, salt and stock or water. Bring everything to the boil and cook fiercely for 10 minutes, then turn the heat down to medium and cook the chickpeas until they're tender – anything from 45 minutes to an hour and a half, depending on how fresh they are. Top up the stock with water if it starts to get a bit low.

For a salad, the chickpeas should remain quite firm. For a casserole or soup, cook them until they are creamy and easy to crush with the back of a wooden spoon.

COOKING DRIED BEANS

Dried beans can be cooked in the same way. Soak them overnight and cook with the garlic, herbs and stock or water as above. Follow the instructions on the packet for the cooking time – it varies enormously with the different types of bean.

HAIRY BIKER COOKING TIPS

. . . .

ROASTING PEPPERS

Preheat the oven to 200°C/Fan 200°C/Gas 7. Place the peppers skin-side up on a baking tray and drizzle them with a tablespoon of olive oil. Put them in the oven and roast for 30 minutes.

Put the peppers in a plastic bag or in a covered bowl and leave them to cool to room temperature. Once the peppers are cool enough to handle, peel off their skins.

PEELING FRESH TOMATOES

Bring a kettle of water to the boil. Score a cross on the base of each tomato, then put the tomatoes in a bowl and pour over the freshly boiled water. Count to 10, then check the tomatoes. If they are very ripe, the skin should easily break and fissure into lines when you insert a knife. If they are less ripe, they may need to stand for slightly longer. When you think they are ready to peel, pour off the water. Leave the tomatoes until cool enough to handle and the skins should slip off easily.

SEGMENTING ORANGES

Take a thin slice off the top and bottom of the orange. Stand it on a flat surface and cut away the peel and outer layer of membrane from the sides, following the contour of the fruit. Take the peeled orange in your hand and hold it over a bowl catch any juice. Cut out the orange segments, cutting as close as you can to the membrane. Take the orange peel trimmings and the discarded membranes and squeeze them into the bowl to get every last bit of juice.

A FEW OTHER NOTES

Peel onions, garlic and other veg and fruit unless otherwise specified.

Use free-range eggs whenever possible. And we always use large eggs in our recipes.

We've made oven temperatures and cooking times as accurate as possible, but all ovens are different so keep an eye on your dish and be prepared to cook it for a longer or shorter time if necessary.

Stock features in lots of recipes and we've included recipes for making your own chicken, fish and veggie stock on pages 314–316. Otherwise, use the fresh stocks available in supermarkets or the little stock pots or cubes. Many are pretty good these days.

RECIPES

· ·

INDEX